Getting Out of God's Way

A Personal Testimony

Reverend Ronald Cole

Getting Out of God's Way
A Personal Testimony

Copyright © 2025 by Reverend Ronald Cole

All rights reserved. No part of this book may be reproduced or transmitted in any form or by any means without written permission of the author.

ISBN 979-8-218-70814-6

Dedication:

This book is dedicated to Joe Ramey. A childhood friend of over 60 years. Joe helped me find my voice in this book and my first book: "Paying Attention: A Spiritual Journey." I will miss our lunches, but our friendship will last forever. I would also like to acknowledge Fred Turner who helped with my first book but passed away before we could start working on this book. He is missed.

The Narrow and Wide Gates

Matthew 7:13-14

"Enter through the narrow gate. For wide is the gate and broad is the road that leads to destruction, and many enter through it. But small is the gate and narrow the road that leads to life, and only a few find it."

Contents

Foreword 1
1 Introduction 5
2 From the Beginning 11
3 The Stage is Set 23
4 Surrendering to the Word of God 27
5 I'd Rather Have This 37
6 Alone in My Solitude 45
7 Is This Really Who I Am 51
8 Did I Do That 61
9 Things Have Changed 67
10 What Do I Do Now? 73
11 Moving Towards the Light 81
12 I'd Rather Have This 89
13 I Am All In 95
14 Can We Really Get Out God's Way? 103
Appendix A 117
Appendix B 121

Foreword

By Reginald Lyles

"O'Lord, make me brave, I pray, in the face of things that terrify and intimidate me and strengthen my heart also, in the face of things that try my patience and require my suffering. So that I might become more wholly dependent upon you in the hour of my trials, I pray this in the name of the one who stands at the right hand of God, interceding for all of the Saints and creation." This simple prayer by W. David O. Taylor, the professor of theology and culture at the Fuller Theological Seminary, is an honest, humble, and brave petition to God for strength for facing the hour at hand.

Many of us encounter moments of crisis and challenges, which, along with the question of "what should we do next," can positively or negatively impact our lives, families, and communities. Flowing through the mind of someone contemplating their situation are often feelings of abandonment, thoughts of inadequacy, and experiences of rejection and failure. Nevertheless, this complex question is frequently filled with fear, doubt, and life-threatening adversity that must be faced. What do we do next?

Certainly, Dr. Martin Luther King Jr. must have felt this way during what is now known as his "Midnight Table Experience," as described in his book, Strive Toward Freedom: The Montgomery Story. It was January 27, 1956, and Dr. King was a 27-year-old preacher in his second year at Dexter Avenue Baptist Church in Montgomery, Alabama. He was a husband and the father of a baby girl. He led the Montgomery bus boycott, and southern racists retaliated with a stream of death threats sent to his home via mail and phone calls. Some say Dr. King received 30 to 40 life-threatening calls each day.

Nevertheless, this one call came at midnight, and Dr. King answered. The voice said, "N-----, we are tired of your mess. And if you are not out of town in three days, we are going to blow up your house and blow your brains out." What should we do—next?

Dr. Martin Luther King got up, went into the kitchen, and made a pot of coffee. He held his head in his hands and loudly prayed, "Lord, I'm down here trying to do what's right. But I am afraid . . . I must confess . . . I'm losing my courage." King says at that moment; he experienced the presence of the divine as he had never experienced before. King says he heard a voice saying, "Martin Luther, stand up for truth. Stand up for justice. Stand up for righteousness. I will be at your side." Dr. King is challenged as to "What he will do—next?" Dr. King says this was a turning point in his spiritual life, and he described it as his most profound and sacred encounter with the Spirit of God.

In the book *Getting Out of God's Way*Rev. Ronald Cole shares a personal testimony about his lifelong journey with the divine. He humbly acknowledges that his relationship with God began early in his life when he was miraculously saved from being struck by a car as a toddler. From the start, he establishes a consistent prayer life, despite his doubts about its power and purpose. Like Jonah, he struggles to believe that God is communicating with him and assigning him divine purposes. Rev. Cole reflects on the critical decisions he faced, pondering, "What will he do next?" He narrates the struggles of an ordinary man who overcame extraordinary challenges, detailing how he succeeded and learned that God is a very present help in times of trouble. He confronts the realities of becoming a teenager living alone, being a teenage father, serving as a battle-tested Vietnam veteran, pursuing an education—including post-graduate degrees—navigating marriage and divorce, raising five children and six grandchildren, and two great grandchildren answering the call to Christian ministry, and recovering from a stroke. Through it all, Rev. Cole learned to trust and obey God by Getting Out of God's Way.

I have known Ronald Cole for over 65 years. Even though we went to different elementary schools, we met as ten-year-old boys competing on the softball field. During junior high and high school, we shared many college preparatory classes as we progressed through our education. Ronald was always a brilliant student and an exceptional athlete who played football and ran track. He was well-liked by other students and was a fantastic dancer—the girls adored him. He genuinely cared about fairness and justice, standing up for those who were vulnerable. He had the courage to take a stand when it was necessary and was willing to fight for what was right. Ronald was not a bully; instead, he smiled and made an effort to befriend others. He appeared to have a maturity beyond his years. I always felt fortunate to have him as a friend.

However, inside of him were issues that he kept private. Ronald lived in a small house in East Oakland in high school with his father. However, his dad was often not in the house, so Ronald mostly lived alone. He had to manage and discipline his daily life as a teenage male when the teenage brain was not fully developed. Consequently, he could be reckless and make bad decisions. Ronald handled his life as an efficient grown man in some areas but was careless in others. He got to school on time, and his homework was completed. However, he consumed too much alcohol. Undoubtedly, it served as a way for him to cope with his isolation and loneliness. Being home alone has its perks and risks. When you are a virile young male popular with girls and having a car, being home alone can result in teenage pregnancy. It did.

Ronald became a teenage father to his precious firstborn Ronetta Cole-Morgan, a wife to Kieth Morgan, and a mother to two: Joshua Morgan, a Navy Serviceman, Petty Officer First Class, and Aaron Morgan, a PGE Supervisor. Ronald later had a set of twins: Ronald Cole and Robin Cole-Fisher, a wife to Narryn Fischer, M.S., and a mother of three sons, Kemit, Kareem, and Kamal. Kemit is attending Amherst College and is a junior playing football. Kareem and Kamal are scholar-high school football athletes and are highly recruited.

Ronald Cole volunteered for the army, to get away from a volatile marriage situation that he felt was going to land him in jail and was sent overseas to Vietnam. Ronald was discharged from the military and returned home, struggling with PTSD and alcoholism. He relocates to Seattle and remarries. He becomes a salesman, builds a family, and constructs a family home. He marries Vicky Cole, and they are blessed with a son and daughter: Reginald Cole, who was a Navy serviceman, Hospital Core man Third Class stationed in Okinawa, and Camara Cole, a mother to Jacob, both of whom are thriving. Jacob is also a scholar athlete and a highly recruited high school football player. These children and grandchildren are evidence of the promises and grace of God, which Rev. Ronald Cole has come to recognize.

This book will encourage readers about the presence and power of God. We all experience doubts and crises in our lives. This book serves as evidence that during times of crisis, a loving God will act as a bridge over troubled waters. It encourages readers to seek God, listen for His voice, trust, and obey. However, one must Get Out of God's way to do so.

Introduction

In the mid-1980s, at the age of thirty-six, I was experiencing significant stress. This raised concerns regarding my health. Aware that stress could lead to serious health issues such as a stroke or a heart attack, I was determined to avoid both. There were five stressors in my life that I could identify: my employment, my marriage, raising children, my desire to progress in life, and dealing with PTSD from my service in Vietnam.

Employment was something I couldn't eliminate; I needed the money working provided. The negative racist environment I worked in contributed greatly to my stress. I felt unable to leave my marriage due to my responsibility to my children, although my relationship with my wife was strained and stressful. In my mid-thirties, I knew I had to continue to grow as a man, father, and provider, which required setting and achieving goals, a process that added to my stress. The PTSD was the cause of constant aggravation. The Vietnam experiences were constantly replaying themselves in my mind, including a firefight where I killed two people, not to mention experiencing racism in a combat zone, which was one of dumbest things I have ever witnessed or experienced in my life. That, coupled with the racism I faced at work created constant triggers.

Those situations were a consistent annoyance. The Vietnam experiences were replaying themselves involuntarily in my mind, throughout my day. To escape these intrusive thoughts, I focused on my responsibilities and goals, leaving little time for relaxation. I was also self-medicating by using recreational drugs and alcohol, further complicating my emotional state.

Figuring out how to control my stress level was challenging. One thing I knew I could do was keep myself in good physical shape. I consistently worked out five or six days a week, knowing from my research that regular exercise helps counter the negative effects of stress.

Having participated in competitive sports earlier in my life, I used that mindset to fuel my drive to accomplish my goals. However, I noticed that while I achieved many goals, they had not been achieved in the way I had planned. Something always changed, and responding to those changing conditions would always cause me stress, whenever I had to modify my plans. Although I knew things did not always go as planned, that knowledge did not lower my stress level. I always wanted things to go smoothly, so I could stick to my plan.

Lack of control over situations associated with my goals caused me stress. Trying to control situations never worked, something always changed without any input from me. The fact that my attempts to control situations never worked did not change my desire to be in control, which conflicted with my goal to lower my stress level. So, I tried to make peace with the fact that I couldn't control things, which took a lot of reflection.

Reflecting on my need for control, I began to question how I had come to believe I was in control of my life. I realized that the guidance and socialization I received from adults and teachers growing up emphasized being a go-getter, self-starter, and independent thinker, traits centered on individualism and self-reliance. This belief led me to assume that hard work and focus would guarantee success. This mindset made me aggressive and focused, believing life was about pursuing what I wanted. Those characteristics were all about being an individual that could stand on his own, which led me to assume I was in control of my own destiny.

When I started reflecting on why my goals weren't being achieved as I had planned, I considered how humans are indoctrinated to believe they are in control of their lives as well as situations they find themselves in. A thought occurred to me, believing we are in control of our lives is part of the human condition. Using our own volition to decide which direction or action to take regarding our lives is also a part of the human condition. So, if that is the human condition, why am I choosing to question the human condition now? My answer to that question was, to question things is also a part of the human condition. This realization made me question whether my stress stemmed from the human condition.

As I reflected further on my dilemma of stress and accomplishing goals, what occurred to me was, some of the things I was told before going out into the world on my own led me into a thinking pattern that helped me to form my self-worth and self-esteem. To build my self-worth and self-esteem, I felt I had to create the individual I needed to be to survive and thrive in the world. While creating that individual, my mind took me in many different directions. Some of those directions were aligned with the Word of God, and some were not. I would like to talk about the many ways I went in different directions and how going in those different directions caused me to get in God's way.

Reading the Bible and occasionally attending church was a part of my life. So, I had some insight into biblical scriptures that stated God is in control, somewhat contrary to my socialization. My socialization was about individualism and building self-worth. So, let me paraphrase what I was learning from my Bible reading, "God is the creator of everything and in control of everything, so if I surrender to and be obedient to the Word of God, God will handle everything, God doesn't need my help." My trying to help God is me getting in God's way.

So, I deduced with my logical mind, if God is the creator of everything and in control of everything, then I should be able to be obedient to God's Word and have everything turn out alright. After putting a plan in motion, I can just continue to take care of business without stressing because God is with me, and in control. I should lean on God, not my own understanding of things. If I believe that God is not a human that he should lie, I can trust the Word of God. I will succeed because I'm trusting in God to do what the Bible says. That removes my faith in myself and my plan, putting my faith in God and God's plan.

This led me to realize that placing faith in myself and my plan was the cause of my stress, because neither I nor my plan were in control; God was in control. I did not know God's plan; I thought I was in control. As my journey continued, I would gain essential insight into the reality that God is in control. My journey gave me the opportunity to see what happens when I place my faith and trust in God. That insight prompted me to reflect on my relationship with God.

Logically, if God is in control, I should trust God and stop stressing. The Bible states, God is the creator of everything, including me and I am created in the image of God. I understand that to mean, I am created in the spiritual image of God because God has no physical presence. The spiritual image of God is at the core of who I am.

As I reflected deeper on what I was learning from my Bible reading, I got the feeling that I needed to pay more attention to God being in control, because if that is true, the human condition and my socialization was also causing me to get in God's way. So, if I have already been created, why did I feel the need to recreate myself? Was it because I did not know the person God had created me to be? Was it because I felt I needed to look outside of myself and assimilate myself into the world? I was unaware that God had already given me everything I needed to succeed and exist in the world, at birth. I believed I had to create a person capable of succeeding in the world. Those beliefs were placing God, the Creator, second to my own thinking. I was leaning on my own understanding and getting in the way of God's plan for my life. Recognizing this, I knew I had to take responsibility for my stress and align myself more closely with God's Word.

My logical mind was telling me, if God is in control, get out of the way, and trust God, there is no reason to stress. Stress problem solved right, wrong; I had done a lot of internal damage by recreating myself. My recreated self, moved me away from the spiritual image of God that I had been created in. Now, I had to do the work to get back to the spiritual image of God within me. To do that, I had to remove old destructive thought patterns and habits I had created while recreating myself.

My goal is to share my journey from the person I created back to the spiritual image of God within me, guided by the Holy Spirit. By letting the Holy Spirit guide me I hoped to see myself as God sees me. To let the Holy Spirit guide me, I had to understand that I was not in control of anything. God states through his prophet Isaiah, "For my thoughts are not your thoughts, neither are your ways my ways, declares the Lord. As the heavens are higher than the earth, so are my ways higher than your ways and my thoughts than your thoughts." (Isaiah 55:8-9) This verse taught me that God's plans are beyond human understanding.

Recognizing this led me to appreciate God's grace, God's unearned favor, which had always been present in my life. The fact that I accomplished goals at all, was God's grace in my life. God's grace is a benefit received by all human beings, whether they believe in the Word of God or not. God's grace is unearned, unmerited favor, which is God's goodness toward those who have no claim on, nor reason to expect, divine favor. The great thing about God's grace is that it is a gift from God. It's important that I understand the saving grace of God.

Before understanding God's grace, I experienced unexplainable, spiritual moments that lingered in my mind, sparking my interest in spirituality. Those moments made me aware of an unseen yet present part of life, deepening my faith. As my faith grew, surrendering to the Word of God and the guidance of the Holy Spirit was something I had to do. After spending years building up my self-worth, self-esteem, and self-importance, I realized, the self-worth, self-esteem, and self-importance, would not serve me going forward in faith. As I surrendered to the Word of God, the version of myself I had created had to pass away, so that the new me, the transformed me, the true me, could emerge. After years of believing I was in control, that was a tough pill to swallow.

More than thirty-five years ago, I coined the phrase "Getting in God's way." Now, I felt I needed a scripture that demonstrates how to get out of God's way. As I searched for that scripture, what occurred to me is I had wrestled with the perfect scripture since my youth. Matthew 6: 33, which states, "But seek first the kingdom of God and his righteousness, and all these things will be added to you."

By seeking God's kingdom and righteousness first, I get out of God's way. If I am busy seeking God's kingdom and righteousness first, I cannot lean on my own understanding, putting me in God's way. My first priority is seeking the will of God, keeping me out of God's way. Achieving God's righteousness by believing in God, and Jesus Christ, the son of God. I take, "all these things will be added to you," to mean, all my needs will be met, and the desires of my heart will be fulfilled.

As I began to associate those spiritual experiences with the presence of God in my life, they took on new meaning. Those experiences had developed in me a desire to understand the spiritual side of life. So, I proceeded under the assumption that I get in God's way by not seeking God's kingdom and righteousness first and that I get out of God's way by doing just the opposite: seeking God's kingdom and righteousness first.

That understanding would have served me well early in life, but perhaps my journey without that understanding was necessary for me to truly grasp an understanding of God's grace and the Word of God. Up until this point I had leaned on my own understanding of things, developing my own way of dealing with things. As I searched for a deeper understanding of spirituality, the importance of leaning on the Word of God and prayer became evident. Proverb 3: 5-6 states, "Trust in the Lord with all your heart and lean not on your own understanding; in all your ways submit to him, and he will make your paths straight." A straight path, while peaceful, requires vigilance to avoid distractions.

This book shares my journey of God's redemption, salvation, transformation and justification in my life. These divine forces changed me forever. Once I truly surrendered to the Word of God and the guidance of the Holy Spirit my old life passed away, I will never be the same. The peace I felt I could have in my life, I have. The stress I was trying to eliminate is gone. As stated in Philippians 4:6 "The Lord is near! Do not be anxious about anything. Instead, in every situation with prayer and petition with thanksgiving, tell your requests to God. And the peace that surpasses all understanding will guard your hearts and minds in Christ Jesus."

So, how do I "get out of God's way"? I think to get out of God's way I have to seek God's kingdom and God's righteousness, being aware of the fact that I am in God's way. Then I can start doing the work to get out of God's way. Join me as I share my experience with the transformative power of God's Word.

CHAPTER 1

From the Beginning

My journey truly began when I realized the importance of committing to be obedient to the Word of God. This realization stemmed from various unexplainable events in my life that I considered spiritual. Throughout my life, I would ponder and reflect on those events, seeking to understand their meaning and how they had impacted my life. Eventually, foresight led me to believe the answers lay in the Word of God.

The first of those events occurred when I was about the age of three years old. This was the first time in my life that I felt protected. My mother had sat me on the porch to wait for my father, who would walk up the street on his way home from work. On this particular day, I got up from the porch and ventured out, walking to meet my father. As I was crossing the street, I heard the screeching of tires as a car tried to stop just before reaching me. I don't know if I was too young to feel fear or if I lacked the awareness of the danger, but I felt no fear as I looked at the front grill of that car. Instead, I sensed a presence- I was not alone. I felt protected. That was the first of several experiences I would have throughout my life. It wasn't until years later, after reflecting on other experiences, that I fully recognized this moment as spiritual.

Although this was not a spiritual event, my father taught me to pray at the age of five. I cannot say I felt a connection to prayer at that age. I feel it was important because I knew nothing of spirituality at that time. My father taught me that essential child's prayer: "Now I lay me down to sleep, I pray the lord my soul to keep, if I should die before I wake, I pray the lord my soul to take. God bless Mommy, Daddy and the whole wide world, Amen." My father was very instrumental in the grounding of my prayer life.

When I lived with him in the third grade at the age of seven, we prayed together every night. For that memory I am very grateful. Although I didn't fully grasp the value of prayer at the time, I cherish those memories. As a teenager, if my father saw me struggling with something mentally, he would just say, "Boy did you pray?" I later came to understand that prayer is not just asking God for things-it is spending time with God.

Upon entering elementary school, the socialization process began. I was encountering different children and adults who were not in my family environment for the first time. I was also attending church and Sunday school with my father occasionally. As well as vacation Bible study during the summer vacation with my sisters. These were the places outside of my home where I was taught fundamental moral principles and the Word of God in my youth. I was taught the ten commandments and to love other people as well as how to treat others as I wished to be treated.

At the age of twelve, after attending vacation Bible school, I sat on the porch outside the apartment where I lived with my family. I was pondering deep questions: Who wrote the Bible? Did they make it up? Could they have made any mistakes? Was Jesus real? Did he truly come from a virgin and walk the earth? (I do not recall if I knew what a virgin was at that age) I can't remember how long I wrestled with those questions before I had my second spiritual experience, but I remember it was before I turned thirteen.

One night I was lying in bed, the room was pitch black. I was struck in the back three times. The blows felt like they went straight through me into the floor. The blows were hard, but painless. I was terrified. I was afraid to look up. I lay there thinking, what had I done? Has the devil come to get me? I lay still, too scared to move. When I finally gathered the courage to look up, I saw lined up on the windowsill, the hats of every branch of military service. I had no idea what this meant. Years later, I recognized it as my first premonition. I would enlist in the military seven years later.

That experience was the beginning of me becoming a seeker. Although I did not know what spirituality was at the time, insight into spirituality is what I would be seeking later in my life. I wanted to know why I had that experience. Being hit in the back in the dark and seeing all those military hats on the windowsill, it had happened, but what did it mean? I would not share that experience with anyone for almost forty-six years. I got out of bed the next morning like nothing had happened.

That second spiritual experience was always in the back of my mind. As my life moved forward, I pondered what I had learned in church and Bible study. So, with the tenets of right and wrong as well as the Word of God in my conscious, I ventured out into the world as an adolescent, where I discovered another set of rules which contradicted what I had been taught regarding right and wrong, as well as how to treat others. I had encountered those contradictory rules before adolescence, but I recall dealing with those rules more intensely when I became an adolescent because I felt accountable and more responsible for my actions. This set of rules was averse to the Word of God, and I would discover as I lived my life that they produced nothing positive, only short-term satisfaction. This set of rules included getting even or revenge, hatred, manipulation, deceit, etc.… I will refer to these characteristics as worldly from this point moving forward.

As life would have it, I had another experience. When I was fourteen, my mother and some of my siblings were moving to Germany with my stepfather, who was in the military. I was trying not to show my anger, but I was devastated. I made one of the biggest mistakes of my life. I remember telling myself there could not be a God; God would not take my mother from me. In anger I stopped praying. I was mad at God.

My attitude was, there is no God. The consequence of that attitude was the first time in my life when I felt truly vulnerable and disconnected. Everything started going wrong. My life deteriorated very quickly. When I say deteriorated, I mean, nothing went right, absolutely nothing. I was constantly late, anxious, and disoriented. I don't recall how long those feelings lasted or how long it took me to identify the problem, but one day at school, during lunch, I wandered off by myself, looking up to the sky, saying, "God I am sorry."

Man, I felt so relieved after apologizing to God. I wondered, had the presence and/or the protection of God been removed from me during that time? I don't know what caused me to feel the way I did, but I never want to feel that way again. I started praying again and have not stopped. I don't remember connecting that event to the blows to my back that night when I was twelve or associating those blows with having felt that presence at the age of three, but I remember coming to the realization that I needed God and prayer in my life.

Though prayer was back in my life, I still struggled with those conflicting values I was learning as I encountered the world. As I went to higher grades in school, and got older, I would encounter situations that caused me to think about worldly ways or Godly ways. When I talk about worldly ways I am speaking of behavior and attitudes that do not acknowledge the ways of God. When talking about Godly ways, just the opposite, this behavior uses the Word of God as its guide and instruction.

When dealing with people, I found myself making the decision to choose a worldly or a Godly response depending on the situation. I felt some situations demanded a worldly response, while others demanded a Godly response. Being spiritually immature, I thought I had a choice; I had not reached the understanding that for a spiritually mature individual all responses demand a Godly response. My journey to that spiritually mature individual would be challenging and rewarding.

My journey towards spiritual maturity truly began once I was out of high school. That was an exciting yet uncertain time. Exciting because twelve years of school had come to an end and uncertain because I had no idea what the future held for me. Unaware of the fact that my purpose had been given to me at birth by my Creator. My purpose, unknown to me then, would be the reason for my life experiences, especially my time in Vietnam. My purpose is the reason for the path I took in life, which is also the reason I live and breathe. My knowledge of my purpose resides deep within me.

The most defining spiritual experiences of my life happened after high school while serving in Vietnam. Those experiences gave us some insight into my purpose. If getting hit in the back at twelve had not truly made me a seeker, the events I experienced in Vietnam certainly did. I would reflect on those events almost constantly for years before receiving any peace.

Three months into my tour in Vietnam, I encountered my next spiritual event at twenty years old. It was a typically hot, clear day. We were patrolling and clearing an area of Viet Cong. I was driving the personnel carrier when a massive black cloud of smoke appeared in front of me, off in the distance. Then the news came over the radio; the Lieutenant's personnel carrier had been hit in the side by a rocket. We had sent foot soldiers out to patrol the area before we drove through the area with the tanks and personnel carriers. The Viet Cong had let the foot soldiers pass them before firing the rocket. Orders were to turn to the right, the direction the rocket had been fired from and fire back. I followed the tank in front of me. As the tank turned to the right I turned to the right.

My sergeant was manning the fifty-caliber machine gun on top of the personnel carrier. He opened up firing in the direction the tank was pointing. Once I stopped, I dropped my driver's seat and grabbed my M-16. I rose up and joined in, emptying a full clip. Then I went back down, grabbed my grenade launcher, came back up and fired a shotgun round, reloaded, and fired a grenade. I did the same sequence about four times, go down, reload then pop back up. I was excited and hyped up, to say the least. The bush was thick so you couldn't see anything but bush. I was shooting to cover areas in front of me. First the area right in front of me, then I'd focus on an area a little further out in front of me.

The fourth time I came up to fire my weapon, I saw my immediate family members (Mother, Father, Sister's, and Brother), faces go across the top of the trees. The images were very vivid, colorful, and smiling. When my stepfather's face appeared (we never had a good relationship, but a gentlemen's agreement that we would not cause any problems) this scared and shocked me. I felt something wasn't right, so I took off my helmet, which left me with no ear protection and crawled to the back of the personnel carrier, where two 60-caliber machine guns were located. I then started firing a 60-caliber machine gun.

There were tanks on both sides of my personnel carrier. As each tank was fired my eardrums would meet in the middle of my head because I had no ear protection after taking off my helmet. When the tank to my right was fired, I was thrown to the left side of the personnel carrier. The tank on the left would fire; I was thrown back to the right side. With machine guns on both sides of the personnel carrier, I would fire one machine gun, and when thrown to the other side of the personnel carrier by the firing of the other tank I would fire the other machine gun. Finally, I unlatched one machine gun and started shooting all around me, even in the trees behind me. I had become disoriented. The firefight ended after what seemed like an eternity!

After the firefight was over, we pulled out looking for kills. The tanks had knocked down trees, which had fallen in front of my personnel carrier. I drove over the trees, I could smell blood, but I could not see anything. A large amount of blood has a very strong, distinctive odor. Once we got past the trees, there was a rice paddy about one hundred yards in front of me. I drove to the rice paddy, turned around, and drove back. As I was driving back, I got the sense that there was something under the trees in front of me. I stopped and told my sergeant there was something under the fallen trees. He called the sergeant of one of the tanks, who had some soldiers come over and move the trees.

Under the trees were two dead Viet Cong. They had been no more than twenty to thirty yards in front of me. They had been hit by the weapons fire from myself and my sergeant. It was an ugly site to see how we had destroyed their bodies. The image of their mutilated bodies still remains in my mind. Many years would pass before I fully understood how damaged I was after standing over the bodies of someone that had tried to kill me, but I had killed them instead.

The fact that the Viet Cong had been right in front of me sent me into a deep rage. After seeing their bodies, I saw a part of me I did not know existed. This was a person I had never seen or known before. Feeling this rage at my core, I never want to see that part of myself again. At the same time, I was making a promise to myself that anybody taking something from me when I got home did not stand a chance. I would do them some harm.

The experience of seeing my family members going across the treetops in color was haunting. I was constantly trying to figure out why that had happened. I had a pocket size King James version of the Bible I would read from time to time when I could get some space for myself. Sitting alone and reflecting, knowing what had happened but not knowing why, wondering if I had seen my family because of the souls of those two Viet Cong rising up to heaven. I am unable to count the number of times I have replayed that incident; it was a constant aggravation for years. I was told long afterwards that the battleground is a very spiritual place. That was a very spiritual experience for me.

About a month went by when I experienced another event. I had been in Vietnam for about four months at this point. My company was returning to the area they were at when I joined them four months earlier. We had to secure the area again, which meant patrolling the area to make sure it was clear of Viet Cong. While riding machine gun on this patrol, I spotted five trails, in the elephant grass, which is over 5 feet tall. The grass was lying down pointing toward the river, so I told my sergeant to call the information in. I was trained to assume that for every trail there would be three to five Viet Cong on each trail.

Our Lieutenant had been removed from the field because there were too many people threatening to kill him. He was replaced with a Lieutenant that had recently graduated from West Point, and lacked field experience, he had been with us for about two weeks. The new Lieutenant told my sergeant, the trails would not be reported to the captain because he did not want to set up ambushes at night. So that meant there were possibly fifteen to twenty-five Viet Gong down the hill from our camp on the river. That made no sense to me. Why should we put ourselves in a vulnerable position by not acting on the information we had gathered while on patrol? The enemy being at the bottom of the hill was not a good situation for us.

The new Lieutenant's irresponsibility made me angry. I did not come to Vietnam to die because of somebody else's incompetence. The soldiers in my company smoked a lot of marijuana at night, me included and consumed alcohol if it was available. Some folks even fell asleep on guard. This guy had fallen asleep while pulling guard on my car one night, so I did not allow anybody to pull guard at night on my personal carrier except myself. I'd do my best owl imitation, straining to see in the dark.

This is when I remembered my older cousins' story. He had been in Vietnam two years earlier as a Marine. His platoon had been warned by reconnaissance not to enter the village by the front gate because the gate may be booby-trapped. But his Lieutenant did not heed the warning. My cousin was behind the Lieutenant when he opened the gate. My cousin said all he remembered was a loud noise. When he woke up, he was in Oak Knoll Navy Hospital in Oakland California with two hundred seventy-five snitches in his body. I was not trying to go out like that.

We were on a reconnaissance patrol, but the Lieutenant wasn't going to use the information we had gathered. It made no sense to me. I was not going to ignore the information I had gathered. To force the issue, I told the other machine gunner to follow me. I unlatched my sixty-caliber machine gun then jumped off the back of the personnel carrier.

Before I could start walking towards the river, within an instant, it felt like as soon as my feet hit the ground, I was hit in the chest by a blow I could not explain. The blow felt just like the blow that had hit me in the back when I was twelve. I was knocked on my back. There was a weight on top of me, something was pressing down on me that I could not see, and I could not get up. I was yelling and cussing for someone to pick me up, but they told me to be calm and relax, they had called a helicopter to pick me up. I was still experiencing this weight on top of me and could only move my head. The helicopter arrived and I was taken out of the field. I thought about what had happened during the flight.

I was dropped off at an infantry's base camp, which was under attack all night. The next day, I was trucked to base camp. On my second day in base camp, I was at the communication shack, and I heard over the radio, "C company at the river in contact." All I could say was "I told them they were there." Then it occurred to me, if I had been allowed to go towards the river, being the first one on the ground, I would have been the first one to draw the attention of and fire from the Viet Cong possibly causing me to lose my life. The thought occurred to me that God had saved my life by knocking me to the ground and not allowing me to move!

Again, something had happened that I could not explain. Unable to forget about those events, or explain them, I would ponder over them for years searching for a meaning. I kept those experiences to myself. Forgetting those events or going without paying attention to them was not in me. Like they say, "God ain't done with you yet." My little King James Bible was always with me, so I would read it hoping to get some insight of any kind with regards to the events I considered to be spiritual happening in my life.

After dealing with the new Lieutenant refusing to report the trails, my trust in my superior officers was gone. I stopped obeying orders and did what I wanted. I was eventually hospitalized because of my behavior. While in the hospital, I was verbally attacked by two white bigots, facing racial slurs, and threats of murder. As I stood in the aisle of the hospital ward, between their two beds, I did not respond to the verbal attack: I was trying to process the situation. That was the darkest moment of my life. I was over 7500 miles away from home, I had lost my hope and vision of a future. I was in a very dark place.

I would look at one then the other, as I tried to process the verbal attack by the two bigots, it occurred to me that I had killed people who were supposed to be my enemy. Yet, these two individuals who were supposed to be fighting that same enemy with me, were verbally attacking me, so they were my enemy. Referring to my military training, which is to kill the enemy, I should kill them since they are my enemy. With that thought in mind I continued my day, with thoughts of accomplishing that goal.

While in the hospital, I was medicated and slept for three days. After not eating, for three days, I was hungry. A nurse was attempting to get me to take some more medication, I was refusing. I told her, "If you can't get me something to eat, you need to get me a chaplain. She contacted the chaplain, who met me in the mess hall(cafeteria). We greeted each other, and he asked me what he could do for me. I opened my mouth to say I was hungry, but instead, I said, "I want to preach!" I was in total shock: That was not what I had planned to say. Afterward, I told him, "I am hungry." That was November 5th, 1969.

The Chaplain got me some mashed potatoes from the kitchen, and after eating, I returned to my bed and took the medication the nurse wanted me to take. I was very perplexed by my statement, "I want to Preach." At some point, I fell asleep and woke up seeing my grandfather in the bed next to me. He had a day or two's stubble on his face which made what I was looking at real to me and he was smiling. Now I am thinking, how can I kill somebody after saying what I said and seeing my grandfather, a preacher in Bakersfield California, I could not kill anyone; I knew what killing the two Viet Cong had done to me mentally. My life would have been over had I gone through with my plan to harm the two bigots. I thank God for that intervention.

Returning from Vietnam, I was stationed in Fort Lewis Washington. I applied for a three-month school drop; it was approved so I got out of the Army three months early. Honorably discharged from the Army in September of 1970 at the age of 21. Life was not the same. Once back in civilian life, I saw the impact military service and the Vietnam experience had impacted me. I had no sense of who I was or what I did. I tried to regain some footing by sticking with my plan to go to school, but Vietnam was constantly on my mind. Having said, "I wanted to preach," was constantly playing over and over in my mind. Peace of mind was not to be had. I considered saying, "I want to preach" to be my calling but I would run from that calling for 40 years.

I remember feeling angry because everybody seemed to be in their groove and flowing with life, but I struggled to fit in and belong, wanting to feel normal. Becoming comfortable with my situation took some time. Finding my way back to a socialized normal, took more time than I would have liked, but that was my reality, I had no choice. I was living a pretty loose life with no roots, no foundation, drinking and drugging just whatever I felt. Then, the promise I made to myself in Vietnam after the firefight regarding someone taking something from me not standing a chance, came into play. This guy took some money from me and about six months later I took the money back. He did not like how I had taken my money back. So, about a year and a half later I found myself in a dangerous situation.

I had dropped out of Junior College and worked at the post office for two and a half years. After ending my employment, I reenrolled in Junior college full-time at 23 years of age. I now had about six months until graduation, close to my 25th birthday. One day, while walking between classes, a guy and a girl got behind me. I did not know they were there. I hear the guy say to me "turn around I'm not going to shoot you in the back." I am thinking to myself, who is dumb enough to turn around to get shot? So, I kept walking until I got to my classroom. Unable to concentrate in class; all I could think about was, whether they be outside when I left class. Upon leaving class I did not encounter them before making it to my car. That incident made it hard to attend class, but I was almost finished with my AA Degree so, I kept attending class.

About three months later, it happened again. They were behind me, but this time I was in an isolated area with no one else around. The guy says something; I do not know what he said. I know I said a short prayer after hearing his voice, "God do not let this guy shoot me in the back." After I prayed, I blinked my eyes, and I was moved. I was in the same general area, but my back was up against a wall. My first thought was to question what had happened, but within an instant I told myself, "If God can do that for you, you can change."

I began trying to change, but any change at this point on my journey would happen slowly. Negative behaviors and attitudes still had a hold of me. I wasn't a criminal, but my thoughts and motivation for doing things were not directed by the Word of God, they were directed by my selfish desires. Attempting to change while I was still struggling with the trauma of Vietnam daily, was very difficult. I desired to do the right thing, but there was a lot of work that had not been done to remove old thought patterns and attitudes. I was still drinking heavily and using recreational drugs. Switching my focus from myself to my three children helped but change still came slowly. Peace was something I longed for, but I could not figure out how to find it.

As I read the Bible occasionally and attended church from time to time as well, making a total commitment to change and surrender to the Word of God was what I needed to do. Almost nightly I found myself having a mental disagreement with God. I would tell God, "You are not talking to me," and God's reply was always the same, "Yes, I am." I was fighting a battle I did not understand nor could I win, but I had not realized that, yet.

CHAPTER 2

The Stage is Set

The next thirty-five years were spent learning what I now call "My lesson." After declaring, "I want to Preach," God and I engaged in a mental tug of war. The conversation was always the same: I would insist, "You are not talking to me," and God would reply, "Yes I am." I was self-medicating with alcohol and some recreational drugs, trying to escape the mental anguish of reliving my experiences in Vietnam.

I continued my education and moved to Seattle, Washington for employment in 1978, after earning my BA. By then, I had three children in California. In Seattle, I married and had two more children. Raising five children across two states, and three households was challenging, but a responsibility I had to shoulder. My marriage ended after nineteen years, just as my two youngest children were reaching adulthood. Once they became of age, I moved back to California in 2001and began focusing my personal development in earnest.

Changing from my worldly ways was a slow process because I was still clinging to certain worldly values, which did not work. Straddling the fence was never going to work, but I couldn't see it then. This was a very frustrating time in my life-I longed for peace but sought it in all the wrong places.

I wondered: Could peace be found in the latest fashions, a new car, a lot of money or a new relationship? I was looking everywhere except within myself.

After ten years of being single, I met a lady who captured my interest. We enjoyed life together, traveling, skiing and scuba diving-activities I had always wanted to try. One day, while sitting on her couch reading the Book of Numbers, I heard a voice in my head say, "I gave you what you asked for; why can't I get what I want?" What I had heard lingered in my mind. I assumed it meant I should do the right thing and marry her, so we married in 2008. Yet, after our wedding, the first part of that statement faded away, while "why can't I get what I want?" haunted me.

Nine months into the marriage, I would get home before my wife, for three months, and wrestle with "Why can't I get what I want?" Reflecting on my life, and the events I had considered to be spiritual, it occurred to me that God's hands were on me the entire time. I had been saved from danger and harm countless times, but I was still honoring the world and not God. Finally, I understood: my mental tug of war with God was not in vain.

This realization filled me with anxiety. I feared that after years of resisting God, God might be done saving me and ready to call me home. Desperate, I prayed, "God, if you give me one more day, I will commit to be obedient to your Word." I think I slept with one eye open that night, trying to make it until the next day. I was full of fear and trembling.

The first thing I did the next morning was call my church and schedule an appointment with the Pastor. I shared my story with him. He had retired so he recommended that I make an appointment to see his son, the senior pastor who had replaced him. Again, I shared my story. He recommended I enter the Ministers in Training program. At the time I was serving as the secretary of the Deacon Board. So, I transitioned into the Ministers in Training program, eager to deepen my commitment.

While my marriage had started strong, I did not want the thoughts and memories of Vietnam to interfere with my marriage, so I sought help from the VA. Alongside the Ministers in Training program, I began a counselling program for PTSD, at the Veterans Administration (VA). I remained open to the help they offered. I knew that replaying the Vietnam experience in my mind daily was exhausting

My social worker and a psychiatrist diagnosed me as having Post Traumatic Stress Disorder (PTSD), a condition characterized by persistent mental and emotional distress, flashbacks, and emotional numbness. They would ask open-ended questions, guiding me to process the experiences. Over time, I noticed that the more I talked, the less frequently I relived those memories. Within a year and a half, the intensity of the flashbacks diminished, providing much needed relief. However, I was still prone to violent tendencies, so I prayed constantly for God's guidance to keep me from reacting to any provocation.

As I replayed the memories of Vietnam less, I became more focused on discovering who I was. However, I noticed a shift in my attitude towards compassion and empathy, which concerned me. I had once felt sympathy for people caught in bad situations, but now I struggled to. Having been in Army Reconnaissance, I had learned that paying attention to one's surroundings was key to your survival. That mindset had become my norm, and I assumed everybody knew to pay attention to what was going on around them.

While counseling at the VA helped, my marriage started to deteriorate. One day, my wife came home from work and announced she had had a change of heart. I stated earlier the marriage started out well but was now falling apart. We separated in 2010, and the divorce was finalized in 2013. During that time, I relied on my faith and therapy to hold myself together. Thank God for the counselling at the VA and my commitment to be obedient to the Word of God.

After committing to be obedient to the Word of God, I realized that my life was not my own. I found myself enrolling in seminary at the age of 60. Returning to school wasn't something I desired, but I knew I needed to study to understand God's Word fully. My study of spirituality was in full swing.

Midway through seminary I suffered a stroke. A blood clot had formed in the area of my brain that controls speech, leaving me unable to talk. Fortunately, I received clot-busting medication within the four-hour time limit, and slowly, my speech returned. Thanks be to God.

The stroke prompted me to retire at age 62 in 2011. I then attended seminary full time, graduating in 2013 with a master's degree in Community Leadership at age 64. However, I was unsatisfied with the spirituality curriculum at the seminary I attended. Craving more depth, I enrolled in a two-year certificate program, in spiritual formation, at Carey Seminary in Vancouver, Canada.

Spiritual Formation I felt was my path to the peace I had long sought. Dr David Currie a Professor at Gordon Conwell Theological Seminary defines it as, "the lifelong, faith-filled process of the Holy Spirit transforming the whole person into the likeness of Christ, to the glory of the Father, as informed by the whole Word of God, in relationship with the whole people of God, to fulfill the whole mission of God." His definition resonated deeply with me.

Dr. Curie's definition of Spiritual Formation encompasses what I feel are the most important aspects of Spiritual Formation, which are life-long, faith-filled, Holy Spirit led and transformative. Spiritual formation is the process of the spiritual shaping and growth of an individual. Spiritual formation is the ordinary maturing of one's relationship with God. Spiritual Formation in my view is the transforming power of the process of surrendering to the Word of God. This process is life-long; regardless of whether that life is short or long, Spiritual Formation is taking place.

At Carey Seminary, I studied the St. Benedictine Rule of Stability, which emphasizes consistency in work, prayer and community. Benedictine monks vowed to remain in one place and with one community for life. There was little flexibility and movement in their lives. As someone that is active and likes to move around, I knew I needed help with stability. The Rule of Stability helped me realize that my true goal was to build a better relationship with God.

Though I wasn't a monk, I adopted aspects of that lifestyle to minimize distractions in my life. From February 2011 until January 2018, I dedicated myself to studying and surrendering to God's Word. My apartment became my sanctuary, where I read and prayed daily, with frequent gym visits to maintain my health. As I grew, my priorities shifted, and I finally embraced the peace I had long been searching for all along.

CHAPTER 3

Surrendering to the Word of God

The solitude of the Benedictine practice greatly aided my surrender to the Word of God, a process that was both challenging and transformative. To surrender means to "give into or abandon oneself to," and to honor my sanctification and the transformation occurring within me, I had to surrender fully to God's word.

My salvation saved me from sin and the consequences of a sinful life, which is separation from God. The transformation within me was profound, changing at my core. As my relationship with God deepened, my heart and interactions with the world changed. The Holy Spirit was moving me to be more Christ-like. Therefore, I had to study to show myself approved. This meant reading, studying the Bible and reflecting on my transformation.

God's Word instructed me to honor my salvation through baptism in the name of the Father, the Son, and the Holy Spirit. Baptism symbolizes the spiritual truths of death, resurrection, and cleansing. Jesus lived and died on the cross for the forgiveness of my sins. Although Jesus died, he rose again, which was God's declaration that Jesus is the son of God, claiming victory over death. My baptism marked my faith and union with God through the death and resurrection of Jesus Christ. This was a baptism by water which symbolized the salvation I have received from my faith in God through the son of God, Jesus Christ. It was a physical sign of the spiritual salvation I received through my faith in Jesus.

This is the life to which I am invited to. My faith unites me with Jesus, and baptism reflects that union. Through this union, I acknowledge the transformation that has taken place within me, becoming a new creation in Christ. As stated in Romans 10:9, "If you declare with your mouth, "Jesus is Lord," and believe in your heart that God raised him from the dead, you will be saved."

My experience with baptism was eye-opening, as I experienced it twice in two different ways. The first time was in 2002, when my youngest son called me to tell me he had gone back to school; had gotten a job and was getting baptized. I was overjoyed by these changes in his life. God knows I prayed for them. I asked if I could be baptized with him. He asked the pastor, and the pastor agreed, so a month later I flew to Seattle and was baptized with my son. That was an enormous blessing for both of us. Although I had gotten baptized, I was not totally committed to the faith in 2002, nor had I totally surrendered to the Word of God, and I was still running from the call I had received in Vietnam.

Seven years later, in 2009, as mentioned earlier after my marriage in 2008, I had an experience that let me know my running days were over. As described, one evening I was sitting on the couch of this woman I was dating, while reading the Book of Numbers, when a voice in my head said, "I gave you what you asked for; why can't I get what I want?" I was sitting there in shock wondering how to process what I had heard. The voice that had said to me while sitting on the couch "I gave you what you wanted" went away. However, the part that lingered was the question, "Why can't I get what I want?" It only intensified. After months of mentally wrestling with the question, "Why can't I get what I want?" and years of wrestling with the "I want to preach" statement, I had made in Vietnam that struggle finally came to an end. I could no longer avoid it.

I recalled the times I could have lost my life but had not. My awareness of God was heightened, which caused me some fear and trembling to say the least. I had not felt that level of fear since walking on my first patrol in Vietnam. The realization that God really didn't have to wake me up in the morning, but he had for many years became very apparent to me at that moment. Solomon says in Proverbs 9:10, "The fear of the Lord is the beginning of wisdom and knowledge of the Holy One is understanding." To that, I say, "Amen."

God had called me in Vietnam November 5th, 1969, and our conversations had continued ever since. But now the struggle is over. No longer could I deny my call. The mental and spiritual tug-of- war going on in my head and soul had ended. Trying to reason away my calling in Vietnam, like I had for the past forty years, was over. No more me saying, "You are not talking to me," and God saying, "Yes I am." God has been relentless in getting my attention and for that I am grateful.

I gave up and gave in to the Word of God. Isaiah 30:21 says it well, "Whether you turn to the right or to the left, your ears will hear a voice behind you, saying, "This is the way; walk in it." I do not know what is in front of me, but I knew what had been to the right of me and the left of me, as well as behind me. The time had come for me to go straight and listen to that voice, "saying this is the way; walk in it." Having chosen to follow the world to the left and the right while ignoring the voice behind me, the voice behind me is now what I follow. That choice has made a big difference in my life. Now, the choices I make in my life don't produce drama and adverse outcomes; they produce peace and express love.

The time had come for me to set aside all of my worldly programming. The Holy Spirit had descended upon me, and I could feel it. I had been baptized in water with my youngest son, but now the Holy Spirit had baptized me. My experience with baptism was enlightening to say the least. Two very different experiences, yet both were very revealing regarding my faith and my relationship with God. The internal struggle within me had subsided, and my life had changed. Jesus states in John 3:5, "Very truly I tell you, no one can enter the kingdom of God unless they are born of water and the Spirit." I had now experienced both.

After genuinely accepting Jesus Christ as my Lord and Savior, the spiritual transformation within me was undeniable. Embracing the new person I was becoming was enlightening. While I remained the same person, my response to the world was different. The anger, pride, and arrogance disappeared. My moral compass was realigned with God's Word. I was spiritually reborn, and the Word of God became the lens through which I view the world. The foundation of my life is now supported by the Word of God; the desire to be worldly has departed from me.

I no longer desire to leave the presence of God for the pleasures of the world, which damages my heart and gives approval to sin. As Matthew 10:39 says, "Whoever finds his life will lose it, and whoever loses his life for my sake will find it." Having discovered my spiritual life in the Word of God, I have turned away from a life of unbelief and disobedience towards a life of faith and submission to the Word of God.

Now, my desire is to offer myself to the Lord with a pure heart, without selfish ambitions or pride. Paul states in Romans 12: 1, "Therefore, I urge you, brothers and sisters, in view of God's mercy, to offer your bodies as a living sacrifice, holy and pleasing to God—this is your true and proper worship." This is not to gain favor in God's eyes but is a genuine act of spiritual worship. My desire is to be used for the glory of God, as I commit to God's Word. I thank God for the grace and mercy that has been bestowed upon my life.

To honor God, I must commit to the Word of God and uphold that commitment. Acknowledging that I cannot return to my old way of living, I have to embrace viewing life and the world through the Word of God. Learning to fully trust and obey is the anchor to my surrender. That's the lens I now chose to view the world through. Understanding that true surrender will bear much fruit with me achieving my goal of a fuller relationship with God. Making me a true branch to the vine, which is Jesus.

God made me in a way that I don't follow anything or anyone blindly. Therefore, I had to study to rightly divide the Word of God's truth to the best of my ability. God's truth is based on God's infinite awareness, understanding, and insight of everything because God created everything. This truth is conveyed through the Holy Spirit. I could not surrender without truly knowing what and who I was surrendering to. I could not submit to the guidance of the Holy Spirit without understanding the true meaning of what the Holy Spirit is saying. God made us all different, so my understanding and perception of things are uniquely my own. I believe God speaks to everyone in a way that each individual can understand.

I want the freedom stated in John 8:32, "Ye shall know the truth, and the truth shall make you free." So, I had to get to know God's truth in order to be able to discern and contemplate on that truth. As I got to know God's truth, I saw it as being personal to me, as I interacted with believers, seeing they saw things different from myself. I begin my understanding of God's truth with John 1:1, "In the beginning was the Word, and the Word was with God, and the Word was God. He was with God in the beginning. Through him all things were made; without him nothing was made that has been made." God is an unseen Spirit that is realized through God's son Jesus Christ. So, I have to believe in and have faith in Jesus, there can be no doubt.

So, I believe Jesus when he says in John 14:6, "I am the way, the truth and the life. No one comes to the father except through me." Jesus is my mentor and when He ascended up to heaven, He left the Holy Spirit to guide me in Spirit and truth. The truth is the essence of God located within me. I get to know that essence by stilling myself internally and allowing the Holy Spirit to reveal itself so I can surrender to its guidance. My faith and relationship with the Holy Spirit have transformed me.

That guidance has to be applied in my everyday life, as I continue to study to increase my knowledge and faith in the Word of God. While enhancing my ability to hear that voice behind me saying, "This is the way, walk in it." This will go a long way in helping me with any struggles I have with temptation and sin. My faith and the Word tell me that I will receive forgiveness if I submit to the Word of God, for we all sin and fall short of God's glory. That's a part of the human condition.

The blessing is in God's Word, so I choose to surrender to God's Word and be blessed. Now my attitude is, Lord, here I am, send me. Whatever God tells me to do, I will do, and wherever God tells me to go, I will go. Knowing I must overcome the battleground of my mind because I am still human. I cannot change my mind unless I change my approach to monitoring my thoughts. Being careful to let the sinful thoughts of temptation pass through my mind and not provoke me to act on them. That is my way of acknowledging the truth of the transformation of my life and God's grace.

Understanding the importance of repentance is a part of recognizing surrender and submission to the Word of God. My belief is true repentance is from the heart. Scripture tells me that God sees everything, but unlike humans, God looks at the heart. I like to think of the heart as the place where the image of God, which I am created in, resides. So, when I repent, my repentance is genuine when it comes from my heart. Halfhearted repentance is not effective. For me when I repented half-heartedly, I would commit the same sin again, but when I repented from deep within myself, I was able to move forward and grow, leaving that sin behind. Not feeling above anything but knowing I'm beyond that particular issue.

The Spirit of God caused that change within me, which I plan to acknowledge for the rest of my life. I know I am a work in progress and will be changing for the rest of my life. Looking to my faith, trusting, and submitting to the Holy Spirit (that voice behind me) takes some getting used to. The pull of the world is always there, but the ability to resist that pull gets easier with the continued practice of faith and trusting the guidance of the Holy Spirit.

Daily practice is necessary for growth, from thanking God for another day to expressing gratitude for keeping me safe throughout the day as I go to bed. Daily I thank God for the grace and mercy placed on my life, knowing that God said he would never leave me nor forsake me. When asked what the most important commandment was, Jesus replied, Matthew 22:37: "Love the Lord your God with all your heart and with all your soul and with all your mind." I see loving God as wanting to please God. What better way to please God than to be obedient to God's Word and the teachings of God's son, Jesus Christ. By loving God and abandoning myself to God, surrendering to God's Word became easier.

My feeling is that to love God I must search for God. I recall reading somewhere, that by searching for God you will find your true self, which I would consider the image of God that I am created in. The mistakes I made in the past don't have to define my present nor my future, I am still breathing so God isn't done with me yet. God is still working on me. Regardless of my circumstances the journey is worth it. God's grace and the guidance of the Holy Spirit will bring me into the light of Christ. That is God's plan to make me more like Jesus, the Son of God.

This is a never-ending journey I am on. My responsibility on this journey is to do the work to get Spiritually (internally) closer to God. After all God is the reason, I am a follower of Jesus. Knowing God loves me, I allow the Holy Spirit to guide me to the person God created me to be. I must trust, with my heart wide open and without fear, and pay attention to what is happening to me, allowing myself to fall into grace.

Grace is the unmerited favor bestowed upon me by God. Something I didn't earn but was given to me because I'm a beloved part of God's creation. This grace provides me the opportunity to know God better for myself, which will allow me the opportunity to discover my true self. What a blessing, to be able to reflect on my past and witness the transformation that has taken place within me. My faith has removed all doubt and fear a non-committed life had produced and replaced it with peace. All because I now have the wisdom to surrender to God's will and have faith enough to follow the Word of God as well as the guidance of the Holy Spirit.

Regardless of my past or my current situation, stepping into obedience and surrender brightened my future. While living as a new creation, I will walk through the remainder of my life as a transformed individual. Expecting my life to reflect my transformed self, displaying the characteristics of the Christian Walk, which I see as humility, gentleness, patience, and love. Each step I take allows my eyes to open wider and my vision to become precise regarding the direction my life is headed. The growth of my faith is evident, and my spiritual eyesight is a lot more profound. My understanding of Hebrews 11:1 which states "Now faith is being sure of what we hope for and certain of what we do not see" is evident.

My faith has become second nature to me, it's like seeing and breathing. It's a conscious part of me, as I delight in the Word of the Lord, persevering in my desire to build my relationship with God and the Holy Spirit. Asking myself along the way, "Am I on God's path or my own path?" Letting the Holy Spirit answer that question as I follow where the Spirit leads me. Not allowing the pull of the present, frustrations of the past or the desires of the future to distract me from my focus of allowing myself to totally embrace my transformation and surrender to the Word of God.

As I embraced my transformation and surrender, I developed the ability and mindset to wait on the Lord. Developing the ability to wait on the Lord took practice and I found it to be a very important practice to develop.

After living a life where I believed I was in control, learning to wait on a Spirit I could not see or constantly feel was difficult. Even after years of this practice, my human nature still wants to move at its own pace. I must constantly remind myself to get out of the way and wait on the Holy Spirit for direction. As stated in Isaiah 40:31, "They that wait upon the Lord shall renew their strength; they shall mount up with wings as eagles; they shall run and not be weary; and they shall walk and not faint." My faith leads me to believe in those Words.

So, I fight the good fight of faith, longing to take hold of the internal and eternal life I have been called to. Still pursuing those characteristics of the Christian Walk, righteousness, godliness, faith, love, endurance, and gentleness. As I acquire those characteristics, I'm distancing myself from my old sinful ways. As I acknowledge the transformation that has taken hold of my life. I use the Bible and scripture as my mirror, because the Bible reveals the God of my transformation.

Following what you can't see or constantly feel is truly mysterious. It's knowing that God is guiding me. Being aware of the presence of God in my life is invaluable, remembering it is God who created me and choosing me to be in a continuous relationship with the Spirit of that creation. That is the essence of a truly prosperous life, being ever mindful of the presence of God. As stated in Psalm 37:4, "Delight yourself in the Lord and He will give you the desires of your heart."

When I reflect on the desires of my heart, they were placed there by the one who created me. What I have learned is, if I practice being in the creator's presence, the desires of my heart will come to pass. I had been trying to acquire the desires of my heart by using my own power and control, only to be frustrated repeatedly. I changed my attitude and prayed, "God, you placed those desires on my heart, so you bring them to pass." I combined that prayer with the practice of being still and waiting on God. My frustration disappeared, and my life became truly spiritually prosperous, enabling me to see the power of my faith. The Spirit of God taught me that I had to get myself out of the way so I could follow where the Holy Spirit of God leads me. This meant that I had to surrender to the shaping and molding that was taking place within me through my sanctification and transformation.

My relationship with God intensified as I grew closer and more aware of God's presence. Like any relationship, there are trials. The trials I experienced in my relationship with God provided me with an opportunity to grow my faith as well as learn basic truths regarding the path God has chosen for me. Sometimes those trials felt like discipline. The Bible says in Hebrews 12:6-7, "The Lord disciplines those He loves, and He punishes everyone he accepts as a son. Endure hardship as discipline; God is treating you as sons. For what son is not disciplined by his father?". What has been created by God, God loves, so I know God loves me.

Any discipline is God providing me with guidance and allowing me to develop the attitude of Paul, which is to be content in all circumstances becoming more like God's Son, Jesus. After all, isn't that the goal of the Christian Walk? To become like and be conformed to the likeness of God's Son? The discipline I experienced taught me who I am and provided me the opportunity to discern who God wanted me to be to claim my position as a child of God and co-heir to the kingdom of God with Christ.

As mentioned earlier, this is a continuing journey because I am a flawed human, and the process of being conformed to the likeness of God's Son is a never-ending process. The importance of this journey are the lessons I have learned along the way with regards to trusting and obeying the Word of God and learning to follow the leading of the Holy Spirit. God longs for my trust and to obediently follow where the Holy Spirit leads me.

The Salvation I received by God's grace is an invitation to rest in God's love and peace. I want to walk with God daily and witness God's awesomeness, while seeing the misery and lack of peace that surrounds me. So, I look to my faith in Christ to overcome the world. I find strength in my faith to overcome the sin that still causes conflict within me. The power of the Word comforts my soul, giving me the healing that transforms me. I am a light trying to shine in this dark world.

God's love and grace are enough for me. My faith says so. So, my daily goal is to rest in God's love and be a conduit for God's love. Letting God's love flow through me to those in my life and those I encounter as I go through life, choosing to submit my life to the one that created it and enter the peace God promised knowing the enemy is defeated.

God's love is real and enlightening. My faith and trust in God's truth humbles me. My humility opens me to allow the work that God has to do within me, transforming me. That is my focus, to let the change within me saturate my consciousness knowing that John 15:4 is true, "Remain in me, as I also remain in you. No branch can bear fruit by itself; it must remain in the vine. Neither can you bear fruit unless you remain in me. I am the vine; you are the branches. If you remain in me and I in you, you will bear much fruit; apart from me you can do nothing." This truth gives me the insight to wait on God, I no longer desire to do things in my own time.

I was created to be in fellowship with God, in the present and for all eternity. When I surrender to God's ways and will for my life, I experience true contentment. Providing me insight into that peace that surpasses all understanding. Spending my time chasing what I felt would bring me fulfillment is no longer appealing, once I learned to go where God leads me, allowing myself to rest in God's loving arms. This is one of the great mysteries of the Christian life.

CHAPTER 4

I'd Rather Have This

My foresight and discernment led me to desire to be faithful to the Word of God. With this realization, I shifted my focus from seeking in the world what I thought I needed to looking within myself for what I truly needed. After spending most of my life looking outward, I felt I had been misled by worldly values. However, I understood that I had to take responsibility for the decisions I had made. As I reflected on my past, I recognized the internal conflict within me, caused by the worldly values I had chosen to follow, that were not aligned with the Word of God.

Surrendering my old self to God and the guidance of the Holy Spirit was an internal journey, with the goal of deepening my faith. Paul says in Colossians 3:5 "Put to death, therefore, whatever belongs to your earthly nature." I came to understand this as letting go of ambitions and desires shaped by my own will. After all, what did I truly know? I had been taught to believe I was in control of my life, yet I realized I needed to give up that illusion.

As I moved towards the truth and the light, I saw that God has a plan for me-one that doesn't require my need for control. So, would I let God lead the way or continue to follow my own path? The answer was clear: I had to let God lead. I had come to the realization that the plan God has for me is just as abundant as the life I envisioned for myself, though it looks different. Worldly abundance- defined by wealth and material possessions-was not the same as Godly abundance. Once I surrendered to the guidance of the Holy Spirit my perception of abundance changed. Now, I view abundance as any and everything God has brought into my life, whether it is, a little or a lot.

The pursuit of worldly success no longer holds importance. I have faith that everything I need will be provided in God's time. This shift signifies my spiritual growth and my ability to look within myself for comfort, rather than relying on external sources. While I still dream and make plans, my approach has changed. Confidence in my ability to make things happen has taken a back seat to my ability to trust the Holy Spirit to guide me. It is not me who does the work, but the God who created me and resides within. I just have to pay attention.

By truly observing God's actions in my life and the lives of others, I know I can trust God. As the saying goes, "He may not show up when you want Him, but He is always right on time." Scripture reinforces this truth: "Be joyful always; pray continually; give thanks in all circumstances." (1 Thessalonians 5:16-18). There are times when it appears the light of the Holy Spirit is not shining, testing my faith. Those are trying times, but those are times when my faith can grow. As I discussed earlier, Jesus said, "He has overcome the world." So, if I approach the world with Jesus as my guide and shield, I will also overcome the world.

Both my victories, and my failures are leading me to my destiny. Knowledge was gained from both, though failures have often been difficult to accept. I can't speak for anybody else, but sometimes it felt as if God was discipling me into submission. I would bask in my victories, only to face the consequences for some transgression, if the victory was won with worldly values. It seemed God never allowed me to get away with anything. To avoid the punishment, the only thing I could think to do was to become obedient to the Word of God and guidance of the Holy Spirit, which took a while. It didn't happen overnight; it was a gradual process.

I now understand that God knows humanity's struggle with total obedience. That's why God sent Jesus, the Son of God, as our mentor. Jesus, the Spirit of God wrapped in human flesh, exemplifies the image in which I was created.

I am the spiritual image of God wrapped in human flesh. This realization led me to seek a deeper connection with God, rather than the worldly image I had constructed of myself. Since Jesus was sent to be my mentor it would only make sense to get to know Jesus. A lot of people know about Jesus and the Word of God, but who is doing the work to truly know Jesus and the Word of God? To know Jesus, I had to study, not just read it, but trust and act upon it. Sounds simple enough, but there is a big difference between knowing and acting on the Word of God as well as trusting in the Word of God. It takes intellect to know the Word of God, but it takes heart to trust and act on the Word of God. Jesus said, "Love the Lord my God with all my heart and with all my soul and with all my mind" (Matthew 22:37). I will trust God. As a man thinketh in his heart, so is he. Proverbs 4:23 states, "Keep thy heart with all diligence, for out of the heart come the issues of life."

Approaching my faith as an athlete, I realized that spiritual growth requires action. When competing as an athlete my mindset was focused on improvement, getting stronger and increasing my endurance. To accomplish those improvements, I had to do the work. I could not go to the gym and look at the weights to get stronger, I had to actually pick the weights up and lift them to get stronger. I could not go to the track and look at it, I had to put my feet on the ground and do some running to increase my endurance. So, to gain a better relationship with God I could not just read the Bible, I had to apply the Word of God to my life and live it to the best of my ability.

As stated earlier, when asked, what was the greatest commandment, Jesus said, "Love the Lord your God with all your heart and with all your soul and with all your mind." (Matthew 22:37) Jesus also said, "And the second is like it: "Love your neighbor as yourself." When I reflect on those two verses my mind is taken off myself, I think about God and others. That shift helps me stay out of God's way. When I focus on myself, I know from experience, I'm going to mess something up. When I focus on God, things just seem to turn out better.

This transformation brings me closer to the person God created me to be. Uncovering mistakes of the past and bad habits I'd formed from worldly living was insightful, but correcting mistakes and bad habits was challenging, but self-discovery is an ongoing process. I now want the Holy Spirit to guide me as my journey unfolds. Being my own guide has not worked out so well and I have no expectation that would change.

Like many, I once pursued money, status, and material things. I was trying to fit in and find my place, being a part of the rat race. But that life left me wandering, much like the Israelites in the wilderness for forty years. I would wander around in this world for forty years before deciding to answer my calling. Although I may have felt in control, I understood that the foundation built on worldly values was very shaky and unstable. My foundation had to be built on the Word of God, which is my truth and is stable. The foundation I had built my life on, based on worldly values, could no longer stand.

To end my wandering, I started to look within myself, worshiping and praising the Spirit of God within me. I removed myself from the rat race by aligning my thoughts and actions with God's values. By changing my focus from an ever-changing world to the unchanging Word of God, I gained stability and peace. Just as God breathed life into Adam, He breathes life into me daily. God can't get any closer to me than the breath of life. It took me a while to gain that understanding, but I want to praise God for the breath of life given me. Without the breath of life there is no me to experience the world. So, I thank God for waking me up to be able to experience God's love.

Now, my goal is to not respond to the world with ego and self-determination, but to surrender to the guidance of the Holy Spirit, which will allow me to get out of God's way. Being an adult at this point in my life I had a good idea of where I began spiritually, where I am now spiritually and where I aspire to be. To get where I aspire to be spiritually, I must remain committed to seeking the guidance of the Holy Spirit. That will require me to change my focus from looking outside myself for what I think I need to looking within myself for what I know I need, which is the guidance of the Holy Spirit. There is also a felt need to contrast between what I think I need versus what I actually need.

When I contrast between what I think I need versus what I actually need, it appears I thought I needed the things of this world created by men to gain the peace and the happiness I am seeking. In reality, what I really need are the things of God already within me. Things in this world get old or lose their appeal and value, so going from one thing to the next thing, believing that was what I needed, I was ever searching but never finding peace. The things of God, which are internal, and eternal, don't change, and never lose their value. Once I understood where my treasure was, the search was over. From that point on, it was about doing the work to know God's Word. Luke states it well in Luke 12: 34, "for where your treasure is, there will your heart be also." I found my treasure in the Word of God and my heart followed.

Doing the work requires total commitment. Being double-minded, wavering between worldly desires and Godly truth, only creates confusion. When I started looking within myself, my perception of things I thought I needed changed. The confusion caused by looking outside of myself became clear. In order to stabilize and stop the confusion I had to make a choice. Would I rather have the peace and stability provided by the guidance of the Holy Spirit or would I rather continue to have the instability of the world? I choose the guidance of the Holy Spirit.

Every day, I see God working around me daily. This realization strengthens my desire to have a relationship with God. My studies taught me that God did not just create and leave me. God's presence remains within me to comfort and guide me. If I surrender to God's presence and follow the guidance of the Holy Spirit, I can count on all the benefits that come with acknowledging and surrendering to that fact. The main benefits are the peace and comfort of knowing I am covered by God's grace and mercy. Surrendering to that mindset is easier said than done, but the benefits are so worth it, believe me.

Why praise the world and external accolades, which are temporary and fade away, when you can praise God, whose accolades are internal and eternal. Once the accolades of the world are gone you have to acquire more stuff or be in a better position to keep the accolades coming. So, if I surrender to a relationship with God, I don't have to continue to acquire stuff and status because I know I have all I need within myself. All I have to do is be faithful to my relationship with God. That's what God desires of me, a relationship that honors God.

A relationship that honors God changed my perception of my worldly ambitions and dreams. My goals are no longer driven by worldly values but by a desire to walk in the light of God. Accepting the fact that I was not in control was a difficult adjustment, but it allowed the Holy Spirit to take over and be my guide. That was an adjustment that was very hard to settle into. My ambitions and dreams were being brought out of the darkness of the world to the light provided by God. This is where one of my favorite verses mentioned before stands tall, Isaiah 30: 21, "Whether you turn to the right or to the left, your ears will hear a voice behind you, saying, "This is the way; walk in it."

I spent years going to the right and the left, ever exploring, never finding the peace I was seeking. After all, I knew as active as my mind was, the answer had to be in my mind somewhere. How could I have all that mental activity and not have the answer to everything pertaining to life? As curious as I was to find the answers to life's issues, I knew I could not figure things out. Even after I surrendered to the Word of God, I often wondered about life's issues. Then I came across a book titled, "Man is not Alone," by Abraham Joshua Heschel. He states, "Curiosity is the state of a mind in search of knowledge, while ultimate wonder is the state of knowledge in search of a mind; it is the thought of God in search of a soul."

Scripture says, "Ask and it will be given to you; seek and you will find; knock and the door will be opened to you" (Matthew 7:7). Is all of my curiosity the Spirit within me leading me to ask, seek and knock? Abraham Joshua Heschel also says, "When mind and soul agree, belief is born." I believe the only way I can get the mind and soul to agree is by turning within. By turning within and allowing my mind to connect with the Holy Spirit within, my knowledge of the creator was increased, and my curiosity was calmed.

As my knowledge of the Creator increased, I prayed. As my belief increased, my faith increased as well. That led me to consider whether there was a difference between belief and faith. Webster describes belief as, "An acceptance that a statement is true or that something exists." Where faith is described as, "strong belief based on spiritual apprehension rather than proof." I have a question: Do you have to believe in something to have faith in that something? Stated another way, can you have faith in something without believing in it? Those questions led me to want to talk about the subjectivity of Spirituality.

Subjectivity is the quality of being based on or influenced by personal feelings, tastes, or opinions. The dictionary describes Spirituality as, "the quality of being concerned with the human Spirit or soul as opposed to material or physical things." While philosophically, the human Spirit encompasses our intellect, emotions, fears, passions, and creativity, I'd like to set the soul apart from those human characteristics and continue to claim it as the place where the Spirit of God resides. That is the subjective nature of spirituality. However, some folks may feel differently.

The soul, in my view, is where the essence of God resides within me. The essence of God are the attributes of God, which are compassion, grace, patience, loyal love, and faithfulness. Those attributes are directed at me, God's creation. Through my study of God's Word and prayer, I became acquainted with this truth. The truth being God is trustworthy. I can count on God to be with me at all times because God is within me.

As my communication with God became more frequent, my faith grew. I did not have to will or intend for my faith to grow; my actions caused my faith to grow. My prayers were coming from a genuine heart, a heart longing to commune with the Spirit of God located at the center of me, motivated by a desire to strengthen my relationship with God. I will praise God with prayers that give thanks for the blessings, asking for the guidance of the Holy Spirit and wisdom to live in God's truth.

CHAPTER 5

Alone in My Solitude

For seven years, from 2011 to 2018, I focused on myself. After retiring in September 2011, I graduated from seminary in May 2013. Inspired by St. Benedict's solitude, I embraced that lifestyle from 2013 to 2018. My socializing was minimal, and recreational drugs were a thing of the past, although I still consumed alcohol occasionally, and would take a couple of puffs of marijuana before bed to help me sleep. I continued counseling at the VA, it was still beneficial. My marriage ended in 2010, and the divorce was finalized in 2013.

For the first time in my life, I had peace. There was no family to manage or children to raise; my children were now grown. My relationship with my children had not changed, I was still Daddy, there for support. Now, my focus has shifted to my grandchildren. I was in a different space, alone, but content.

This solitude gave me the space to reflect on and embrace the transformative power of God in my life. I took full advantage of this time, feeling grateful for the experience. As I aged and matured physically, I also sought spiritual maturity. As my spiritual journey unfolded, I came to understand that the amount of peace and stability I desired could be measured by the amount of attention I gave to the presence of God. When I focused on God and the teachings of Jesus, my life became peaceful. Reflecting on my past, I saw a stark contrast between a life with God and a life without God. The life my spiritual journey was leading me to was eye-opening and very rewarding.

After committing to be obedient to the Word of God and entering seminary, I realized the importance of grounding my understanding in scripture. It was necessary that my understanding begin with God's Word as stated by Moses in the book of Genesis. Beginning in Genesis 1:27 states, "So God created mankind in his own image, in the image of God he created them; male and female he created them." In the Bible's creation story, Adam and Eve were created by God. It is stated God created them in his own image, I interpret this as a spiritual image rather than a physical one, as God has no physical form.

So, the spiritual image of God exists within all humanity. God, being the loving Creator (father/mother) cared for them and all their needs were provided. God gave them dominion over the earth and placed them in the Garden of Eden, where food was plentiful. They did not have a worry in the world, but under one condition: that they had to be obedient to God's Word and not eat the forbidden fruit, which grew on the tree of knowledge of good and evil. That makes me wonder, does humanity have the same opportunity to have all their needs met if they are obedient to the Word of God?

The serpent appeared and approached Eve. Appealing to her curiosity, he convinced Eve to eat the forbidden fruit, and she offered some to Adam, which he also ate (and told God that "The woman YOU GAVE ME made me eat the fruit" accepting no responsibility for his own actions). Genesis 3:7 states, "Then the eyes of both of them were opened, and they realized they were naked; so, they sewed fig leaves together and made coverings for themselves." Could this be a metaphor for them realizing they had free will?

They disobeyed God when they ate from the Tree of Knowledge of good and evil. It is widely believed that sin entered the world through the actions of Adam and Eve. From that point on, man has been born with the disposition to sin. Man can ignore the Word of God and use the free will God gave him to do his own will. Is this when we begin to get in God's way?

Studying the Israelites deepened my understanding of obedience and consequences. My understanding of the Israelite's disobedience enlightened my understanding of the transforming power of the Word of God. The Israelites were in the land of Canaan, a land given to them by God, referred to as the Promised Land in the Bible. A famine occurred in the land of Canaan, and there was no food. God had used the deceitfulness of the brothers of Joseph to send Joseph to Egypt ahead of the Israelites to prepare a way for them to survive. When Egypt became oppressive to the Israelites, God took them out of Egypt.

God protected the Israelites from their enemies. God used a pillar of cloud to lead them in the daytime and a pillar of fire to lead them at night. All their needs were provided; they received water from a rock to drink, mana, and quails as food to eat, but still, the Israelites complained. Even though God provided for them and took care of them, they chose disobedience, and the punishment for their disobedience followed. Their punishment was to wander in the wilderness for 40 years and not enter the Promise Land.

Reflecting on my own life, I saw similarities to the Israelites. God provided for me, but I often ignored God's presence, believing I was in control. Like them, I wandered in my own wilderness until I realized I needed to listen to the Holy Spirit within me. I could no longer ignore the calling I first expressed in Vietnam: "I want to preach."

The Israelites were loved and cared for; their needs were met, but they were disobedient, which was followed by punishment. The pattern is not rocket science, disobedience followed by punishment. In the Old Testament, God, through the prophets, told Israel they would be punished for their disobedience; it was not a secret. Moses and the prophets warned Israel regarding their disobedience.

The prophets also shared God's promises with Israel. Having read the Bible from cover to cover, many times, at this point in my life, I appreciate the promises of God. The meaning of promise states, "a declaration or assurance that one will do a particular thing or that a particular thing will happen." According to Bible Gateway, a website I like, there are 5467 promises in the Bible. It would seem 5467 promises would cover everything. It is stated in the book of Numbers 23:19, "God is not a man, that he should lie; neither the son of man, that he should repent: hath he said, and shall he not do it? or hath he spoken, and shall he not make it good?" Does God promise and not fulfill?" I believe that God does not mislead and will always deliver exactly what the

Word of God says. I thought I was in control, but I came to the realization that the light of the Holy Spirit within me is to be my guide and in control.

So, as I studied, I recognized the need to break my habit of disobedience. Not knowing or understanding my purpose, reflecting over my life, I could see how I had looked outside of myself for what I thought I needed. As I began to understand the Word of God, I arrived at the understanding that there was a guide within me that would lead me to a righteous path away from sin, towards obedience.

Like the Israelites, I did not pay attention to what God had done for me, by protecting me and providing for me. There were moments when I faced danger and injury but somehow, escaped both. I believed it was my own ability or my cunning that kept me safe. So, just like the Israelites I wandered in the wilderness. I wandered in my own wilderness until I realized I needed to listen to the Holy Spirit within me. I could no longer avoid what I said in Vietnam, "I want to preach." I had to answer my call.

A New Testament promise that resonates with me is Romans 1:16-17, "For I am not ashamed of the gospel, for it is the power of God for salvation to everyone who believes, to the Jew first and also to the Greek. For in it the righteousness of God is revealed from faith for faith, as it is written." Salvation is the cornerstone of my faith, because it is this knowledge that convicts me. I have been provided a way to connect with the indwelling image of God within me. And how did I get here? Faith in the Son of God, Jesus, got me there.

As mentioned in the introduction, the scripture I felt would help me get out of God's way is Matthew 6: 33, "But seek first the kingdom of God and his righteousness, and all these things will be added to you." When I stopped struggling with that scripture and embraced its truth, my focus on God became constant. I no longer needed proof of Jesus' existence—I had faith. The fact that I could not see God or Jesus no longer mattered.

Focusing on my faith is what I had to do. As stated earlier in Hebrews 11:1, "Now faith is the substance of things hoped for, the evidence of things not seen." I felt the need to discern between the meaning of faith and belief. Belief is the acceptance that something is true or that something exists, and faith is complete trust or confidence in someone or something. It was hard for me to see how I could have one without the other. I had to believe in God before I could have faith in God

As I continued studying and reflecting, I could see God's discipline had shaped me. As stated earlier in Hebrews 12:6, "Because the Lord disciplines the one, he loves, and he chastens everyone he accepts as his son." The realization that living outside of the Word of God came with a price, occurred to me. The truth is, I wasn't aware of that price until I started paying attention to the Word of God. I thought trials and negativity were just a part of life, unaware I could change my focus and change my life. Comparing a life of obedience to a life of disobedience made all the difference in the world. It was like someone turned the lights on; God requires me to be obedient to God's Word as stated in the Bible so I can benefit from its teachings and receive the promises of God.

What I've shared above is what I base my faith on. I believe I am created in God's spiritual image and disciplined when I use my will to contradict the will of God. I believe the Spirit of God comes through the Bible, even though it has been touched by man many times. The Bible, as an acronym is, Basic Instructions Before Leaving Earth. I have watched my life change for the better, just by getting out of God's way and being obedient to the Word of God.

CHAPTER 6

Is This Really Who I Am

Attending seminary was both informative and challenging. As I studied intensely and practiced stillness, the foundation of my faith took shape. As I constantly reflected on my past, questions that had lingered in my mind for years regarding spirituality and faith were now coming into focus. I could now compare my life before surrendering to the Word of God, to my life after surrendering to the Word of God.

It was important that I understood the person I was and how I had come to be that person. As I reflected on my life, I saw how my life experiences and emotions had shaped my personality. Both life experiences and the emotions I felt, had influenced decisions I made regarding my life. Before surrendering to the Word of God, my focus had been on surviving and thriving in the world. I made decisions I felt would enhance my ability to survive and thrive, but now I questioned whether that truly defined me.

So, with that in mind, I continued my self-examination and reflection. As I reflected, I asked myself, "Is this the effort it takes to discern between the good and evil within me?" The good being the part of me that honors God and the evil being the part of me that does not. Do not get me wrong, everything that does not honor God is not evil; I said it that way for simplicity's sake. I wondered, is this something everybody struggles with as they encounter life and search to find their purpose?

In my youth, I had no understanding of being created in the spiritual image of God. Though I knew the Genesis creation story, my understanding of the importance of that story was lacking. So, I will share that scripture again, Genesis 1:27 states, "So God created mankind in his own image, in the image of God he created them; male and female he created them." I did not possess the spiritual maturity, insight, or discernment to look within myself for the image of God I was created in.

It occurred to me that, of all God's creations, humanity seems to struggle with its identity. How I had chosen to identify myself provided me with direction and meaning. While interacting with the world, the way I viewed myself was determined by what I based my identity on. I could base my identity on how I looked or who I knew, or the clothes I wore. My personal identity could be rooted in my occupation, level of education, gender or ethnic background, and many other characteristics. An understanding of my identity was developing within me that was enlightening. However, I was beginning to realize that basing my identity on worldly values was deceptive. Once I reflected on my personal identity, I could see how my identity was not based on God's truth.

This realization led me on a journey of self-discovery, seeking the spiritual image of God within me—my authentic self. Searching for and embracing my authenticity became a powerful and transforming journey. I arrived at the understanding that every person is uniquely created in the spiritual image of God, with a purpose. As people, we are all unique, there is no one else on earth like us. God is in the creation business; he is the potter, and we are the clay. Along with our uniqueness comes our purpose, but how do we get to know the purpose for which God created us? I believe that by getting to know our authentic selves we get to know our purpose.

Basing my identity on things of the world was not my authentic self. While studying in seminary, my true authentic self-began to come into focus. A prayer by Augustine, an early church father from Carthage, North Africa, who was a very important figure in the fourth-century church, whose teachings created a theological system of thought that had a lasting influence on theology, gave me insight. Augustine's prayer was, "Grant, Lord, that I may know myself that I may know thee." What I hear Augustine asking God, is for the ability to know himself so he may know God, which is his true self. I can't remember where I heard it said or who said it, but it's a short prayer that I feel compliments Augustine's prayer, "Lord, help me to see myself as you see me."

Stated another way in the words of C. S. Lewis in the book titled "Mere Christianity," "Your real, new self… will not come as long as you are looking for it. It will come when you are looking for him." In my view, I find him (meaning God) where the Holy Spirit lives, deep within me. I realized that true self-discovery required a relationship with God, who knows me better than I know myself. I want to look at my life through the lens of the Holy Spirit, so I can see my purpose. I owe it to myself and the God who created me to know my true God- created self. Having a unique destiny to fulfill and role to play, I can't fulfill that destiny or play that role without discovering my true identity.

Reflecting on my youth, I realized a significant part of my identity was being formed while attending school. School is where I encountered diverse personalities and viewpoints, because I began to interact with people outside of my family. These experiences influenced my perceptions and reactions, molding me over time. Relationships, both positive and negative, left lasting impressions, and my understanding of them evolved as I matured. My reactions to those situations shaped who I was becoming.

This was a time in my life when I developed relationships and learned life lessons from those relationships both positive and negative. The impact of those lessons and relationships stayed with me for a long time and my understanding of those lessons and relationships changed as I grew older and matured. Often, other life lessons prompted me to reflect on previous lessons and adjust my life and attitudes according to my current situation. As I reflected, I recognized how maturing and growing older had impacted my life.

As I grew older, I observed my friends going in different directions, and I began to decide which direction I wanted my life to take. I began to pay attention to older people and what they were doing and had done in their lives. I observed the results of their actions, some negative, some positive and asked myself, do I want the same results for my life? This was a big part of my maturing process. I started to separate myself from the crowd and started developing the strength to stand alone.

When I mention developing the strength to stand alone, I'm talking about having the strength to separate myself from the pack and follow a direction that was truly on my own path, ignoring peer pressure. There was another pressure waiting for me regarding the direction I was choosing. This pressure was, would I choose a path determined by Godly values or the world? Would I choose the pleasures of the world or the Word of God?

For me, early in life, the temptations of the world were attractive. I had a rebellious streak, and I was an adrenaline junkie as well. I sought excitement, feeling the need to test limits and boundaries at times. In my youth, I chose to interact with the world and the ways of the world. Though I had been taught right from wrong in church, the world's temptations pulled me away from those teachings. The struggle between worldly values and God's truth created internal conflict.

I've heard it said that it's your perception of things that makes them right or wrong. People perceive things differently, so their perceptions of right and wrong can vary. What one person may perceive as right another person may perceive as wrong. Is that because one person is following the Word of God, and the other person is not?

As stated earlier, attitudes that I perceived to be worldly were revenge, greed, hate, slander, manipulation, etc... When I reflect on those attitudes, I don't recall, from my own experience, them ever producing any peace, only negativity and drama. There were two lenses through which I could view the world, one being a Godly lens, and the other a worldly lens. The lens I used would determine my perception of the world around me. Using my God given free will, I could choose which lens I would view the world through.

In youth, I often saw through a worldly lens, but as I matured spiritually, I recognized the peace that came from viewing life through God's perspective. Decisions made with a Godly lens brought peace, while those rooted in worldly values led to chaos. As I grew spiritually and matured in my faith, there came a point in my life when the lens I chose mattered. My preference is for the peace produced by my Godly lens over the drama produced by the worldly lens. I wanted more insight into why I had chosen the worldly lens, which prompted me to consider my environment and socialization.

Socialization shaped my thought processes and desires, but as I matured, I developed needs and aspirations independent of my upbringing. My cultural group was a determining factor in my socialization. My personality was formed and molded as I accepted or rejected the beliefs and attitudes as well as the social norms of my environment. Once I embarked on my personal journey, I developed needs and desires, independent of my environment. My Uncles were my role models growing up. Due to family dynamics, they were not educated. I saw the negative impact that had on their lives and chose to make education a priority in my life.

As I developed needs and desires, independent of my environment, I was recreating myself. I felt I had to be my own creator. I had no understanding of the fact that I had already been created in the spiritual image of God. My focus was to create an image of who I thought I needed to be to have the ability to survive in the world. However, I was becoming aware of and starting to grow in an understanding that I did not need to redo what God had already done! I needed to seek God so; I could find out who God created me to be and from that understanding I would come to know my purpose.

To find my purpose, I had to seek the spiritual image of God from which I had been created. The Spirit of God, that resides within me. It is when I sought that spiritual image of God within my soul that I found my true self. As I continued to study and reflect, I grew in the understanding that, searching for myself outside of a relationship with God, was not going to result in the truth I was seeking. With that understanding, I no longer wanted to live the untruth I had created by recreating myself. For me to view myself as anything other than God's creation was not to see my true identity. So, I continued my self-examination and reflection to build a relationship with my true self, by seeking God first.

There was something within me that needed to know why I felt the need to be the work of my own hands. I didn't understand that creating a life based on worldly values was not the truth and was pulling my heart away from God. Little did I know, if I built my identity on the rock, (Jesus Christ) which is my God- centered self, I would be building lasting peace and contentment in my life. I had to stay faithful to the Word of God. The worldly life I had created, produced temporary peace or satisfaction within myself. However, that temporary peace or satisfaction was based on worldly values such as materialism, possessions, insincere relationships, or corrupt activities I found myself involved in. That type of peace faded away so, I would have to buy something new, get a new activity, or new relationship to recreate that temporary peace.

My self-examination also revealed that my talents and blessings were gifts from God, not products of my own making. My ego had led me to believe otherwise. I had convinced myself that I was in control and could take care of my needs better than God. I developed an ego which is described as, "a person's sense of self-esteem or self-importance." Believing I was my source, not understanding that God was the source of those attributes, not me and my EGO. I thought I had to help the Lord out by putting some "me" on my life. However, the Scriptures teaches, "If my people, who are called by my name, shall humble themselves, and pray, and seek my face, and turn from their wicked ways; then I will hear from heaven, and will forgive their sin and will heal their land" 2 Chronicles 7:14. I had to humble myself and acknowledge God as my source.

To put some "me" on my life I felt the need to develop a personality and EGO that I thought would lead me to the desires of my heart and enhance my ability to survive and thrive. I have heard it said that EGO is, "edging God out," and as I reflected on that, I could see in developing my personality that I had incorporated some of God and some of the world in that personality. The worldly part of me got in God's way. I could justify my actions with selfish rationalization: God wants me to be happy. That is the part of me that made me think I was in control of things in my life. The more I felt the need to control, the less I truly surrendered to God.

As a human, I have control issues. Those control issues are really trust issues. The less trust I have in God, the more I feel I must control things. I came to understand that I had not created myself and that I was not truly in control of my life. Those control issues were hampering my ability to truly surrender to the Word of God. The scripture I struggled with was Luke 18:17, "Truly I tell you, anyone who will not receive the kingdom of

God like a little child will never enter it." Digesting that scripture was hard but necessary. True surrender required childlike faith, something I found difficult as an adult who thought I had life figured out. When a child is born their eyes are covered by a film, but once that film is cleared by a natural process the child can see clearly.

When a person is born again in Jesus Christ their spiritual eyes are covered by the film of the things seen and experienced in the world. This film is removed by a spiritual process called sanctification that comes from studying the Word of God and being obedient to God's Word. I had to approach the Word of God as the new creature in Christ that I had become, with wonder and awe as a child.

My commitment to my relationship with God had to be done with Spiritual integrity, no half stepping. Spiritual integrity begins with faith in God and is enhanced by being in love with God. Spiritual Integrity is described as: the state of being undivided together with the quality of brutal self-honesty. It demands a considerable depth of self-awareness and an uncompromising willingness to be authentic. To be authentic I had to deny the worldly person I had created and speak truthfully from my God-centered soul. No matter what the situation, Spiritual Integrity would have me speak my truth.

Having finally chosen to answer God's call, I now hungered for a more committed life to the Word of God. So, priorities had to be established that would allow me to spend more time getting to know God. Finding my way to building a solid relationship with God, with all of the mental stuff I was dealing with took focus and intent. I was still attending the VA counseling and had come to deal with the PTSD effectively. I kept my focus by continuing to practice the concept of Benedictine stillness.

The good fight of faith had to be fought. This meant learning to actively wait on God. When I mention actively waiting, I'm referring to studying, meditating, fellowshipping, and praying while watching God move in my life and the lives of those around me. The Holy Spirit must be allowed to possess my heart and lead me to the perfect will of God, replacing my will and selfish desires. Allowing this transformation to happen within me has brought blessings into my life, bringing me closer to God and to that peace that surpasses all understanding. As stated earlier, in Philippians 1:6, "Being confident of this, that he who began a good work in you will carry it on to completion until the day of Christ Jesus," and I believe that!

With that in mind the EGO I had built could not stay in place. My choices and attitudes toward life and people could no longer be determined based on what I felt would enhance my survival and ability to get what I wanted out of life. My worldly reactions to the world, which were constantly changing and prompting me to use worldly values such as revenge, dislike, or hatred, manipulating and other negative reactions to things I did not like when I would encounter them, had to be discarded and replaced with Godly grace, understanding, patience, perseverance, forgiveness and love.

With this new understanding I had to allow the Holy Spirit within me to transform the person I had created. This transformation was not easy. The person I felt I needed to be to survive and thrive had lost his appeal because what the attitudes of that person were based on could not stand. My created self was being replaced by my God-created self. I was losing that feeling of being self-sufficient and in control while coming to realize the impact the Word of God was having on my life.

I felt I was starting to lose myself because my old self was coming to know the truth. The things I had founded my identity on were being replaced by the truth within me. The things I found security in no longer felt secure. It was in losing myself that I felt I had found my true self. I was gradually dying inside while coming alive. Dying to self is not easy, but the benefits were worth it. Dying to self-brought me face to face with my truth. Letting go of my self-made identity felt like losing myself, but in reality, I was finally finding my true self.

As stated earlier in Matthew 10:39 "Whoever finds their life will lose it, and whoever loses their life for my sake will find it." My understanding of that scripture is, if I hold on to the life I had created based on worldly values I would not find my spiritual life, but if I let go of my worldly life, I will find my spiritual life. Jesus, the Spirit of God wrapped in human flesh sent into the world to be a mentor and sacrifice for all humankind is pointing the way. I felt a weight lifted from me as I grew in that understanding, Jesus said his burden is light. I now believe that because of the changes that have taken place in my life.

The stress and anxiety I use to feel when confronted by change or a challenging situation are gone. I now have the wisdom to be still internally before reacting. That stillness allows me to wait and watch things unfold, staying out of the way. From a spiritual perspective that makes sense to me, because to see myself as anything other than God's creation is to make light of my Creator and not give light to my true identity.

If God created me in God's spiritual image, but if I continue to get in the way, I will miss out on my blessing. That blessing being the Holy Spirit within me looking after me, guiding and protecting me to the fulfillment of my needs and my destiny. It is well stated in Matthew 6: 33 "But seek first his kingdom and his righteousness, and all these things will be given to you as well."

The Holy Spirit plays such a necessary and crucial role in my life. I look within myself and through the eyes of the Holy Spirit to see who I was created to be and the purpose for which I had been created. Until I took the time to develop and nurture a relationship with the Holy Spirit within me, I was unable to grasp my purpose. To avoid shooting in the dark I had to surrender to the guidance of the Holy Spirit within me and allow God's revelation to open my eyes to my purpose and true identity.

As I looked at life through the lens of the person I had created, I could see God's grace in my life. To show God my gratitude for that grace, I had to faithfully seek God. To faithfully seek God, I had to change, and that change had to be based on being obedient to the Word of God as presented in the Bible, which was a different motivation from my previous motivation to survive and thrive in the world. This changed my decision-making processes. My mindset was moving from a me-first mentality to a God-first mentality. A mental space where I accepted that I had been created in the spiritual image of God and needed to focus on that as my foundation, versus looking outside of myself to form my foundation on an image I had created.

That changed how I viewed life, which changed how I viewed the challenges I had faced in my life. The challenges I encountered throughout my life were now seen as God's way of shaping my identity and attitudes into the person I was meant to be. No matter how I reacted to a challenge, whether with a negative or positive attitude, I am being led to where God wants me to be, because God is in control of everything. These challenges provided me with an opportunity to gain insight into God's movement in my life and grow my faith in the Word of God. I now wanted to see myself as God sees me and to understand my purpose.

I know I could have benefited from that kind of insight earlier in life, but I had to get my lesson. It occurred to me that if I did not get my lesson regarding a particular experience, making the same decision when facing that situation again, I would be allowed to experience the situation or challenge again until I got it right. I knew to call on God when I was challenged with different circumstances and situations in my life, believing God was my resource, now I understand that God is my source, not a resource.

As I continued to reflect on my past, contrasting my life before surrendering to the Word of God with my life after surrendering to the Word of God, it was easy to see a life with an identity and foundation based on Christ, produced a different result for me. My life was now producing a peace that lasts and does not fade away. The steadfast love of the Lord is now my security; God's love never ceases nor changes. As stated in Hebrews 13:5, "…Never will I leave; never will I forsake you." God is the same yesterday, today, and forever. Jesus is now the cornerstone of my identity and the foundation of my faith. The journey to my true self continues, but now I walk with confidence, knowing that my identity is rooted in God's eternal truth.

CHAPTER 7

Did I Do That

Accepting responsibility for my actions—especially my responses to the world around me before surrendering to the Word of God, was essential to my sanctification. There could be no excuses or finger- pointing. The devil did not do it, I did it! Whatever choices I made, I was responsible for them. By taking responsibility, I was able to discern whether my responses were driven by worldly reactions or godly intentions. Reflecting on my decisions helped me understand how the person I had created was either aiding or hindering my ability to follow and surrender to God's Word.

In my youth, I lacked wisdom and self-control. I let my mind do the talking while I blindly followed, often walking straight into situations I later regretted. Then I would get mad about the way things had turned out. To avoid taking responsibility for my actions, I would blame everything on the world. My mind wasn't the problem, the world was. Then I would usually create more problems for myself when trying to use the free will bestowed upon me by God to get out of whatever problem I had created.

There was a felt need for me to understand who I was and how I came to be that person. It was necessary that I take responsibility for creating a person other than the person God had created. This was all part of my journey. As I reflected on my journey, it was obvious that I had been striving to accomplish things using my own strength, leaning on my own understanding as well as the free will bestowed upon me by God. Through my discernment, I realized that the struggles and challenges I faced were often the direct result of this self-reliance.

Many times, my understanding did not honor God, the true source of the peace and fulfillment I was seeking. Once I accepted the fact that most of my trials had been caused by steps I had taken outside the will of God, my faith was able to grow. I realized that when I lived apart from the Word of God, I was unknowingly wandering, regardless of the plans and goals I was trying to accomplish.

Having plans and goals was a good thing, but I was now concerned about whether those plans, and goals were supported by the will of God. I had to know the Word of God to be able to determine whether my plans and goals were supported by the will of God. As I studied and got to know the Word of God, I began to understand the will of God. Getting to know the will of God caused my attitude to change regarding things not going my way. Now, rather than getting upset, I would look within myself and reflect on what had happened. It was a completely different experience from looking outside of myself to find blame for things not going my way, I began to grow spiritually.

Self-reflection before reacting gave me a better understanding of the consequences of walking outside the will of God. I realized that the lack of peace in my life was a direct result of straying outside the will of God. Yet God was patiently waiting for me to turn my heart and mind inward because God loves me. By not being mindful of the path God had laid out for me, I was unable to hear the voice of the Holy Spirit, missing out on the guidance the Spirit provides. That was an error I had chosen to make.

To make different choices, I needed a different mindset. Jesus says in John 16: 33, "I have told you these things, so that in me you may have peace. In this world you will have trouble. But take heart! I have overcome the world." This verse revealed that no matter which path I chose—God's or the world's—problems would arise. However, I was beginning to view those problems differently, once I chose to surrender to my conversion. Rather than becoming upset, I sought to uncover the lessons within my challenges. My stress lessened, which was significant since stress was one of the burdens I longed to release.

Now I view stress as a mental issue created by my own thoughts. I had not thought about stress in that way before. My mind and the thoughts generated within my mind, were the problem. Some thoughts just pass through my mind and some thoughts just linger and prompt me to act. Some actions align with God's will; others do not. As I studied and my faith grew, I developed a better understanding of the negative thoughts that were outside the will of God and the positive thoughts that were aligned with God's will. My ability to discern which thoughts led me closer to God and which led me astray increased as well.

There was a lot going on with me mentally. I was still dealing with PTSD from my Vietnam experiences. Staying busy helped quiet my restless mind. I was questioning the way things were and why things were the way they were. My goal was to use everything God had given me to find the peace of mind I sought and felt I deserved.

My mind is where my perceptions of the world around me are formed. The environment I was raised in played a big part in the perception I had formed regarding the world around me. I found this aspect of my life very interesting because people form opinions about others based on the environment they come from, and I knew people formed opinions about me because I was a Vietnam veteran.

Many Vietnam veterans are suffering and did not adjust well once returning home, I was determined not to be one of them. One incident occurred where a guy approached me and said, "Because you've been to Vietnam, you think you are owed something." I will not repeat what I told him but when I finished speaking, he knew my truth. My goal was to go in an entirely different direction. I knew I could work and accomplish whatever I wanted.

Searching for my own path and purpose, I recognized how my upbringing had influenced me. Although I loved some of the adults in my life, I didn't care to pattern my life after theirs. It took a lot of work to undo the influences they had on my life, but I felt the work was worth it for my children's sake. I did not care for my children to see a lot of the things I had seen growing up. I had seen a lot of domestic violence and anti-social behavior growing up.

Perhaps this was God's grace guiding me through the Holy Spirit to make better choices.

Through studying God's Word, I realized my discontentment had started in my mind. Questioning and criticizing the world only fueled my frustration, leading to anger and negative reactions. Such attitudes weren't healthy—mentally or physically. To become whole and healthy, I had to change those negative attitudes and actions. Sanctification transformed my outlook, and I am grateful for God's grace, which granted me the wisdom to change. The journey towards my truth became a lot easier.

Recognizing the darkness in negativity, I saw how it affected my inner being—the image of God within me. I believed the light should dominate my inner being, not the darkest. To overcome the darkness, I had to become attracted to the light, which I believed could be found in the Word of God, because God is the light. Moving towards the light became easier when I acknowledged that I had walked in the darkest long enough, and knowing the outcome of that journey, which did not attract the peace I was seeking.

Why remain oppressed by the darkness when the truth of the light is available? As stated earlier, "The truth will set you free." It became obvious to me that I was hindering my relationship with God by continually wandering off the path God's Word provided. By wandering off of God's path was inhabiting my ability to produce anything of lasting value. As mentioned earlier, when it comes to wandering off of God's path, I turn to Isaiah 30:21: "Whether you turn to the right or to the left, your ears will hear a voice behind you, saying, "This is the way; walk in it." After living my life going to the left or the right, I knew that feeling. Discernment led me to say, "been there, done that," I had grown and gained some wisdom.

Now, the light is more attractive than the darkness, giving me the opportunity to get to know my true self. As I discerned and contemplated on the light and my true self, the consequences of walking outside the Word of God became even clearer. As spoken by Jesus in John 14:6, "Jesus saith unto him, I am the way, the truth, and the life: no man cometh unto the Father, but by me." Therefore, I needed to take my clue from Jesus, the Spirit of God wrapped in human flesh, the same Spirit in which I am created. It is God's desire for me to understand that God is the light and the way.

God created me to love me, and if I chose my own will over God's, my life would reflect that choice.

That understanding gave me insight into the fact that many of my trials were the result of me walking outside the will of God. External things cannot bring internal peace. I stopped deceiving myself and faced that truth. Which is, if I continually walk off of God's path and do not pay attention to the pain I am causing myself, I will continue to wander aimlessly, not knowing or understanding my own foolishness.

God will not be mocked; I reap what I sow. As stated in Galatians 6:7-9, "A man reaps what he sows. The one who sows to please his sinful nature, from that nature will reap destruction; the one who sows to please the Spirit, from the Spirit will reap eternal life. Let us not become weary in doing good, for at the proper time we will reap a harvest if we do not give up." I remember what the old folks used to say, "a hard head makes a soft butt." God wouldn't let my disobedience go unchecked, there were consequences for my behavior. Reflecting from another point of view, which was, all of my trials were not the consequences of worldly behavior. Some of my trials, I believed, were sent to me by God to prepare me for my personal journey. Those trials coupled with my own created trials would shape me into the person God created me to be. It is important that I pay attention and get my lesson, the same trouble will keep presenting itself until I get my lesson.

So, when trouble comes, I can look to Jesus and the Word of God for peace. I walk in the light with the Word of God, because I know that trials are a part of my journey. I know the Holy Spirit will guide me through the trials. Peace cannot come from walking in the darkest. The light will lead me to a personal and intimate relationship with God, as I lean on my faith.

Faith offers me the ability to watch God change things and reveal a deeper truth than what I can see on the surface. God can reveal the light in situations that appear to be dark. As my faith has grown, my ability to discern has grown as well. Spiritual discernment is the Holy Spirit guiding me to help me arrive at the best decision. I have found discernment to be very comforting because when things are challenging, I can lean on my faith, knowing the Holy Spirit has my back and will guide me. The Holy Spirit is a good friend to have, because life can and does change in an instant.

CHAPTER 8

Things Have Changed

As I mentioned in the introduction, change caused me stress. As someone who always has goals and plans, I frequently faced change. My goals were achieved, but rarely in the way I had envisioned, because things always changed. I would adjust to the new conditions, relying on my own power and insight before I knew to ask God for guidance.

During this time, I coined the phrase "getting in God's way." God is in control of everything, including the changes I experienced, and yet I still achieved my goals. If I was going to achieve my goals regardless of changes, why stress? So, I should "stay out of God's way" by not inserting myself into situations.

With this insight, I learned to be still and lean on God through prayer, and listen to that voice behind me saying, "this is the way; walk in it," for it was God that had changed things. Since the mid-1980's, I have been trying to figure out how to get out of God's way. After years of trial and error, as well as leaning on my own understanding, I believed I could find the roadmap to stay out of God's way, in the Word of God.

Changes in my life would offer me different alternatives to choose from. Learning to discern between a Godly path or a worldly path, I choose God's path. Developing this skill helped me to focus on the things of God rather than the distractions of the world. Once I consistently chose the Godly path, the Word of God began to dominate my life, transforming my life for the better.

My perception of things changed. I thought my age gave me wisdom, but I soon realized how little I truly knew. What I knew had little meaning in the big scheme of things. The internal battle between God and myself ended after I committed to be obedient to the Word of God. Now, when I stop to rest, our internal battle does not begin; I can actually rest and reflect if I like. No longer am I saying, "You are not talking to me." God is talking to me, and I am listening! After forty years, I'm no longer trying to outrun God. My life has changed.

I can recognize darkness around me, but there is no darkness in my life. Negative relationships are not allowed to take root in my life. I am achieving my goal of being a positive mentor for my grandsons and consistent positive influence on my family. The woman that has entered my life is a true blessing. Providing the support, I need to continue growing and achieving my goals.

My primary focus is sanctification and remaining true to the grace God has placed on my life. Salvation has freed me from the temptations of this world, allowing me to move toward the person God intended me to be. I am gaining the mental strength to embrace my uniqueness while losing the desire to conform to worldly standards.

Sanctification is leading me toward the truth and life Jesus' spoke of. Salvation has given me the wisdom to put God first, ensuring that no external circumstances come between us. Now, I understand that I can place all circumstances at the foot of Jesus and be still, knowing that they are taken care of. If there is a lesson in this circumstance, I will learn it. This was another instance where I was getting in God's way, believing I had to solve every problem myself. My mind would start working overtime trying to figure out a solution, but now, with my understanding of prayer and stillness, I allow my mind to rest, avoiding unnecessary stress.

Salvation has changed how I handle challenges. In my younger years, I viewed stressful situations as battles to be won. I reacted pridefully, standing up for who I thought I was, putting my ego out front. Now, I see stress as a hindrance to my peace. Acknowledging my salvation, I have placed the Word of God at the forefront instead of my pride. As salvation took hold of my life, I realized that my true self was never the prideful man I had been. I had always been a guy that desired peace, but being caught up in worldly living, I did not know how to acquire that peace. I should have tried Jesus first, but it is said, "Don't should on yourself."

I know pride has caused me to think more highly of myself than I should have. Pride also caused me to be defensive at times, defending the allusion of the person I thought I was, being easily offended, prone to overreaction. Once I surrendered to the Word of God and my transformation things were different. The values of the world no longer mattered. What mattered was me doing my best to live my life according to the word of God. I no longer needed to be defensive, and I am not easily offended. My practice of stillness was really beneficial when it came to letting things of the world pass by.

Another change I noticed as I went through the sanctification process is, I was putting God first, and my level of humility had increased. I was being transformed! The part of the world I was dealing with did not support humility. To be humble meant, I had to place a low value on myself, which does not work in a "me first," society. The world seems to reward the prideful, confident individual, not the humble one. However, my selfishness had subsided; everything was no longer about me. Although I had not been a totally selfish person, now putting the feelings of others before myself was more noticeable to me. I embraced humility and welcomed the opportunity to prioritize the well-being of others.

Surrendering to sanctification was not easy. I am human, with an active mind. Nevertheless, God created me and was faithful to me, so why shouldn't I be faithful to God? While I struggled to give up my worldly ways, God was there being faithful, allowing me the time I needed to break through to the light. There was only one way for me to breakthrough to the light, I had to believe in Jesus Christ the son of God.

Dying to self was the most challenging aspect of building my faith in Jesus and the Word of God. Letting go of the person I had created did not happen overnight. It was difficult, but I believe the goal of building a relationship with God was worth the effort. As mentioned, earlier, trusting in the scripture, Philippians 1:6 which states, "Being confident of this, that he who began a good work in you will carry it on to completion until the day of Christ Jesus," was very helpful. I trusted that the Holy Spirit would guide me through my transformation.

As my belief and faith in God grew, the misconceptions I had regarding life, created by my old self, began to fade. My ability to see the light and the truth increased as I leaned less on my own understanding and more on the Word of God, guided by the Holy Spirit. A verse that comes to mind is Proverbs 3:5-6 which states, "Trust in the Lord with all your heart and lean not on your own understanding in all your ways, acknowledge him and He will make your path straight."

By building a relationship with God, sin lost its appeal, and temptation lost its power. God's holiness began to take root within me, changing my interest and desires. Things I once did I no longer wanted to do. I began to choose the light over the darkness. Looking outside of myself, living through others, and following the crowd lost its appeal. I learned to respect my uniqueness and search for my purpose. I continued to reflect on my past, trying to gain an understanding of the contrast between my pass with my present. I no longer wanted to be a stranger to my true self.

The human mind seeks to know why, what, and how. Could I discover who God created me to be in a day, a week, or a month? I believe it will take a lifetime. We are all a work in progress, growing through the seasons of life—childhood, adolescence, adulthood, and old age. I believe God reveals himself differently at each season of life, each season building on the last. I would like to think that my knowledge has grown with age, making me wiser.

Should wisdom lead me to understand that God doesn't need my help? After all, God is the Creator of all things. If God created me, do I need to help the Creator, believing I could improve on God's creation? This is where faith comes in. My faith reassures me that God doesn't need my help, God needs my obedience. The more faithful I become, the more obedient I will become. Increasing my ability to, "Be still and know that I am God." Even while being active physically, I am able to still myself internally.

I have stopped trying to micromanage God and manipulate people or situations to fit my desires. Things no longer have to go my way. Trusting in God's timing and ways has strengthened my faith. As my faith increased,

I witnessed my focus changing, becoming aware of the spiritual gifts I was blessed with. My character has transformed from worldly to Godly. Where I once walked proudly in my worldly values, I now have the strength to walk humbly with Godly values. I am learning to walk with God as the person God created me to be.

CHAPTER 9

What Do I Do Now?

What I desired was the guidance of the Holy Spirit, but there was another Spirit that wanted my attention as well, that is the Spirit of temptation. Temptation is the adversary that is opposed to the Word of God; some call it Satan, some call it the devil, I call it temptation. Temptation's purpose is to tempt me to act in ways that are contrary to the Word of God. Although temptation is an irritant, I can use my reactions to temptation to gauge my level of my faith and obedience to the Word of God. If I give into temptation, I am not doing so good. If I stand firm with the help of the Holy Spirit and resist temptation, I am winning.

Temptation tries to convince me that it would be much easier to keep doing what I have been doing, which is living outside of the Word of God. Temptation knows that by winning the battle of the mind, the heart can be changed. Romans 12:2, states, "Do not conform to the pattern of this world, but be transformed by the renewing of your mind. Then you will be able to test and approve what God's will is, God's pleasing and perfect will." Therefore, I must guard my mind, which is focused on living a life rooted in the Holy Spirit within me, to guard my heart. Changing the direction of my life has required hard work. While I am busy redirecting my free will, increasing my prayer life, and practicing stillness, temptation is constantly knocking at my door. So, I lean on Proverbs 4:23, "Guard your heart with all vigilance, for from it flows the issues of life."

So, daily I have to use my free will, to choose God's will for my life, and resist the temptation to remain worldly. I had to give up worshiping the god with the little "g," which was me. That is an error I can no longer afford to make because it causes me to walk outside of the will of God, which causes consequences I do not like. My struggle is to not stray from God's path and expose myself to the unprotected dangers of the world. Through my studies and life experiences, I know that God loves me and is patiently waiting for me to turn my heart and mind to God. That knowledge helps to strengthen my resistance to temptation.

As I grew spiritually, my reaction to the world changed and I moved away from things I once did. That was not to temptation's liking. So, I had to stay on the lookout for temptation's deceptive ways, trying to lure me away from the light and the peace-filled life provided by being obedient to the Word of God. A scripture that speaks to my situation is 1 Corinthians 10:13, "No temptation has overtaken you except what is common to mankind. And God is faithful; he will not let you be tempted beyond what you can bear. But when you are tempted, he will also provide a way out so that you can endure it."

My trials and difficulties are now viewed differently. Before, I saw them as a challenge or distraction; I now see them as an opportunity for me to grow. My trials and difficulties do not define me; I use them to refine myself. This refining leads me closer to my goal of attaining a better relationship with God. I have become more mindful of my spiritual journey. The doubt and resistance to the guidance of the Holy Spirit have subsided. Temptation and sin have lost their power and appeal. My ability to follow and be obedient to the Word of God has grown.

Turning a blind eye or deaf ear to the guidance of the Holy Spirit is a mindset I can no longer entertain. Looking within myself where the Holy Spirit resides, for guidance, has become a welcome habit. The Holy Spirit has changed my beliefs and increased my faith, giving me the ability to look away from temptation. Having gained the ability to see the trials temptation has caused me, has brought a clearer understanding of the meaning of, "leaning on our own understanding." It was my free will and understanding that I was following, not the will of God.

The pull of the temptations of the world have lost their power over me, and certain anxieties have faded away. Cravings of the flesh and other worldly desires look and feel different to me now. As I mentioned before, my perception of things has changed, and I approach them differently now. Anxiety regarding my future has changed, after all, what do I have to be anxious about? I follow Jesus, who said he "has overcome the world."

The stronger my commitment to the Word of God as the truth became, the more successful I became at resisting temptation. I had to respond like Jesus did when he was tempted by the devil and say, "it is written." Every time the devil tried to tempt Jesus, He would state, "it is written," referring to, it is written in the Word of God. As stated in Matthew 4:4, Jesus answered, "It is written: Man shall not live on bread alone, but on every Word that comes from the mouth of God." So, I knew I would find my anchor and my support in the Word of God. Walking by faith is not easy; and changing my outlook on life and my priorities has not been easy. However, it has been worth the effort.

Relying on my faith and God's grace, placed me in opposition to the world. I am covered by God's grace; my faith is protected. I can stand firm and confront the temptations of the world. My heart is purified and sanctified by my faith, giving me the spiritual character and integrity to renounce the ways of the world. By renouncing the ways of the world, I move away from worldly pursuits towards holy pursuits. Temptation wants me to keep my holy pursuits a secret because that way temptation can keep me in solitary confinement. Just me, temptation, and my holy pursuits, that is darkness. I want to break free of the darkness and move towards God and the light, by speaking openly regarding my Godly pursuits. That reminds me of John 3:30, "He must become greater; I must become less."

My faith and love for God grew as I applied the perseverance needed to change my old habits, becoming more persistent at applying God's Word to my life. God's grace and mercy in my life became more evident to me. I began to sow seeds that glorify God, building my life on the foundation of truth. That was the result of my studying God's Word, seeking God in prayer, and fellowshipping with other believers for support. Church attendance was no longer from time to time, I was in church every Sunday.

After years of solitude and practicing stillness, I became convinced that the essence of God resides in my soul, where the Spirit and image of the God who created me resides. The attributes of God, compassion, grace, patience, loyal love, and faithfulness are directed at me, God's creation. I've learned to direct those same attributes towards humanity and nature. It's through my study of God's Word and prayer that I became connected to this truth: that God is trustworthy. I can count on God to be with me because God is within me. As mentioned earlier, God said, "Never will I leave you, never will I forsake you." Hallelujah!

Even though I am a sinner saved by grace, when I sin and I will sin, I acknowledge my fall from grace, and ask for forgiveness, knowing I will be forgiven. God sees everything, so why not confess and repent? I can't truly move forward until I deal with whatever the sin was, because my relationship with God is similar to my relationships with others, the truth always comes to the light. Keeping secrets and living half-truths only leads to unsuccessful relationships, and that applies to all of my relationships and primarily with God.

Offering myself to God with a pure heart is what is desired of me by God, free of selfish ambition and pride. My desire is to honor God for the grace and mercy that has been placed upon my life. Again, I share what Paul states in Romans 12:1, encouraging us to offer our bodies as living sacrifice. The scripture states, "Therefore, I urge you, brothers, and sisters, in view of God's mercy, to offer your bodies as a living sacrifice, holy and pleasing to God—this is your true and proper worship." This is not to gain favor in the eyes of God, but rather as an act of spiritual worship; my desire is for God to use me for God's glory and kingdom building.

Letting that voice within me guide me, I know to pray and be still internally. Praying knowing God will answer the prayer in God's own time and in God's own way. God's grace is sufficient enough for me, there is no need for worry or stress. My charge is to increase my knowledge and understanding of God's Word and apply it in every circumstance. As stated in 2 Timothy 2:15, "Study to show thyself approved unto God, a workman that needeth not to be ashamed, rightly dividing the Word of truth."

That brings to mind a visit I made to Tulsa Oklahoma after becoming a Deacon at Allen Temple Baptist Church. I was visiting Aunt Reen, a country preacher. She heard that I had become a deacon in my church. So, during a discussion, I forget the subject, she says to me, "What did God say in Isaiah boy?" I read the Bible regularly, but I had no idea what she was talking about. After replying I don't know, she says to me, "Baby, you can't understand the New Testament unless you know the Old Testament." That statement grounded my reading of the Bible. From that day on, when reading the Bible my intent was to study the Old Testament so I could understand the New Testament. Now, when reading the New Testament I understood when the Old Testament is being quoted and the context from which the quote came.

This is not a quote, but it has always given me food for thought, so I will mention it again. When asked what the most important commandment was, Matthew 22:37, Jesus replied: "Love the Lord your God with all your heart and with all your soul and with all your mind." Also as stated before, I see loving God as wanting to please God and what better way to please God than to be obedient to the Word of God and the teaching of Jesus Christ. By loving God and abandoning myself to God, surrendering to the Word of God was made easier. I thank God for the grace and mercy placed on my life daily, believing what God said, "he would never leave me nor forsake me."

Recalling what C.S. Lewis said, "Your real, new self… will not come as long as you are looking for it. It will come when you are looking for him." So, to love God, I must search for God. I will find my true self, which I consider to be the image of God that I am created in. Regardless of my circumstances, the journey will lead me to a better relationship with God. God's grace and the guidance of the Holy Spirit will bring me into the light of Christ. That is God's plan, to make me more like Jesus. As stated before, the mistakes I have made in the past don't have to define my present or my future. I am still breathing so God isn't done with me yet. He is still working on me; I am just one of God's masterpieces.

Knowing I am on a never-ending journey, my responsibility is to do the work to get spiritually (internally) closer to God. After all, God is why I am a follower of Jesus. Knowing God loves me, I allow the Holy Spirit to guide me to the person God created me to be. I trust, with my heart wide open, and without fear, paying attention to what is happening to me, and allowing myself to fall into grace.

Grace, as previously mentioned, is the unmerited favor given to me by God. Something I did not earn but was given to me because I'm a beloved part of God's creation. It provides me with the opportunity to know God better for myself, which will allow me to discover my true self. What a blessing, to reflect on my past and see the transformation that has taken place within me. My faith has removed all the doubt and fear that a non-committed life produced. I now have the wisdom to surrender to God's will over my own will. I now have enough faith to follow the Word of God and the guidance of the Holy Spirit, to the best of my ability.

If I continue to acknowledge the Holy Spirit's presence within me, I know I can trust in the promises of God. God's love and grace are enough for me, and my faith affirms this. Therefore, my goal is to rest daily in God's love and be a conduit for God's love. Letting God's love flow through me to the people in my life and those I encounter as I go through life. Again, I choose to submit my life to the one that created it and enter the peace God promised knowing the enemy is defeated.

My faith gives me freedom from the one that is in the world. Free to experience the fruits of the spirit, which are love, joy, peace, patience, kindness, generosity, faithfulness, gentleness, and self-control as described by Paul in Galatians 5:22-23 which reads, "But the fruit of the Spirit is love, joy, peace, forbearance, kindness, goodness, faithfulness, gentleness and self-control. Against such things there is no law." My trials still present themselves but my approach to dealing with them has changed because of the growth I have experienced in practicing God's truth. Where I used to stumble through the difficulties placed before me, coming to understand God's grace, has removed the stumbling and given me the ability to walk straight.

Accepting God's grace as truth is key to staying connected to the vine, which is Jesus Christ. Jesus states in John 15:5, "I am the vine; you are the branches. If you remain in me and I in you, you will bear much fruit; apart from me you can do nothing." Being still and knowing that I do not have to evoke my own will in a situation is important. What I need to do is hold up my end and watch God do the rest with grace. God led me to it, and God will lead me through it; when God leads, I win. When I reflect on my life and compare the times when my ego was leading versus when I let the Holy Spirit and grace lead, the difference is amazing. My ego's leading produced drama and discontent; the Holy Spirit produced peace and love. It doesn't get better than paying attention and reaping the benefits of my newfound knowledge.

My newfound knowledge gave me insight into my situation. I had been focusing on the outward appearance of things instead of the condition within me. Matthew 23:25-26 spoke to my situation, "You clean the outside of the cup and dish, but inside they are full of greed and self-indulgence. First clean the inside...and then the outside also will be clean." I could no longer allow external things to impact my life in a way not pleasing to God. What I believed others would think, could no longer be my focus. My focus had to be to follow the truth within me.

Once I understood that, I knew the peace I had been seeking had always been within me. All I had to do was to be faithful to the Word of God and allow God's grace to transform me into the person God had created me to be and the inside of my cup became clean. By allowing my transformation to take place, I had become a new creation. Then I gained insight into the understanding that my transformation would not end until my journey in this world is over. It is all a part of the sanctification process.

Giving up my old life was not too much to ask for receiving the consciousness to be aware of the benefits of God's love and grace. I now truly understand that I am a child of God. Scripture assures me that God will complete the work he has begun in me. The Word God spoke regarding me would not return void but will accomplish the purpose for which God spoke it. The love and grace of God is a gift I can never repay, but I can share it with those whom God puts in my path.

CHAPTER 10

Moving Towards the Light

Settling into the truth of God's Word often felt overwhelming. My greatest challenge was removing the darkness from my mind and heart, caused by years of relying on my own understanding. This darkness hindered my desire to walk in the light of God's truth. After many years on a worldly path, my willingness to change had to align with the results I wanted. I desired daily awareness of God's presence, which required a consistent effort to change my long-standing attitudes and perceptions shaped by worldly thinking.

These attitudes and perceptions were established by my interactions with the world and adopting worldly values. The desire to be accepted and to belong to certain groups, led me to adopt or accept the values of those groups, which were not always aligned with the Word of God; that was peer pressure. Internalizing these values caused confusion when deciding the direction of my life. This was a pivotal time in my life when I was making the decision to stop turning to the left or the right and start listening to that voice within me saying, "This is the way; walk in it."

That was when I truly understood the importance of submitting to the will of God. I learned to, "Get out of God's way," allowing God to do the work of transformation within me. My tendency to do things with my own will, had subsided to a great degree. By seeking God first and inquiring of God through prayer, made it less likely that I would encounter trials caused by taking steps outside of the will of God.

When I did face trials, I used to discern between my worldly walk and my walk of faith. By relying on the Word of God and the guidance of the Holy Spirit, I gained clarity. Through both a worldly lens and a spiritual lens, I could see which path produced the better outcomes for my life. As stated in James 1:2-4, "Consider it pure joy, my brothers, and sisters, whenever you face trials of many kinds, because you know that the testing of your faith produces perseverance. Let perseverance finish its work so that you may be mature and complete, not lacking anything." Perseverance was absolutely necessary to go through the different challenges I encountered, and my faith deepened through it.

The hardest challenge for me was letting go of the belief that I was in control and gaining the understanding that I had never been in control in the first place. This is where the Benedictine practice of stillness and solitude helped me the most. I was not socializing a lot which helped with my ability to focus on my control issues and gain better clarity. I did not have new people entering my life that I had to build a relationship with. My social circle was small, mainly consisting of my children, their children and old friends.

As I discerned more deeply, I realized that the worldly education I had received was misguided and foolish. My understanding of the character of God increased, and in seeking the truth, I saw the love and grace God bestows upon what God has created. I was being transformed by the renewing of my mind. My desires changed, seeking acceptance from the world was no longer important. My goal now is to please God by glorifying God's name, in the name of Jesus.

Prayer and studying God's Word is my focus. I continue to embark on a path of reeducation, unlearning old ways and discovering a different way of approaching life and the world. That requires an uncompromising commitment and persistence to change my habits and mindset. I had to ask myself, "Am I up to the challenge?" Would the amount of time it takes me to change depend on the length of time I had spent living a worldly life? Foresight gave me the insight that this is a lifelong journey, so as long as I have life in my body, I have time to change.

That type of commitment meant staying focused, constantly reminding myself that change was what I truly wanted. I want to move forward in the truth by building my foundation on the Word of God, using Jesus Christ as my example. This meant pressing forward, even when doubts arose, and I felt tempted to quit. Having the Word of God as my road map is different from the world being my guide. Where I used to think I was working things out for my good, I now have the mindset that understands and believes that God is in control and works things out for my good because I love God. So, I can get out of the way and watch God do what God does because God is always present. I am made in God's spiritual image, so God is always deep within me.

Have you ever heard the phrase; "God is not done with you yet"? Or, "I'm a work in progress"? Both of those, in my view, speak to the fact that walking with God is a lifelong journey. Think about it; some of us are called to begin our conscious walk with God earlier than others, while some receive more life lessons than others before turning to Him. Everyone's journey is different. I, for one, would have preferred to skip some of my life lessons.

Reflecting on my past, I realized that many, if not all, of my trials had been caused by my thinking, lack of faith and the inability to turn away from temptation. I was paying attention to the wrong god, myself, with a little "g." I believed I was in control. I wasn't looking within myself, where God resides, but outside of myself at the world. The "me" I had created was not the me that God created. The me I had created was in God's way. God created me to worship God not myself.

Worshipping God means being obedient to God's Word. And being obedient to God's Word requires work. That work, for me, was changing my habit of disobedience into a habit of obedience. This process, known as repentance, is asking God to forgive my disobedience. It demands persistence and perseverance to change old habits, something I asked God for in prayer.

I cannot share this scripture enough; Jesus says in Matthew 10:39, "Whoever finds their life will lose it, and whoever loses their life for my sake will find it." This verse helped me see that the life I had built, based on worldly values, was unstable, shaky, and not based on truth. By giving up that life and submitting to God's Word, my foundation is now solid. This solid ground is the Spirit of God that is within me, the image of God, I was created in. I have gained the ability to wait on God for guidance, looking within myself for God's direction.

The "I got this" attitude faded away. I no longer react impulsively to situations but instead allow the Holy Spirit to guide me. Old habits are being transformed as I continue to pray, study, meditate on the Word of God. My old self is fading away as I get accustomed to my new self, my true self that God created me to be. As Paul says in Galatians 2:20, "I have been crucified with Christ; it is no longer I who live, but Christ lives in me….." And as my faith continues to grow, I am assured that I have God's hedge of protection surrounding me.

John 16:33 reminds me that Jesus has overcome the world for me: "These things I have spoken to you, that in me you may have peace. In the world you will have tribulation (trouble); but be of good cheer, I have overcome the world." I spent time reflecting on this and now accept that Jesus has already figured out the world for me. What I need to do is stay out of the way and pay attention to the Word of God as spoken by Jesus.

Reaching that state of mind was worth the time and effort it took to get there. Everything happened in God's time. My change could have occurred in an instant, overnight or it could have taken days, weeks, or years, even a lifetime. As I grew more proficient at listening to God's voice, my character shifted. The arrogance of the world faded, and my understanding of humility deepened. Humility is no longer seen as weakness, but as a virtue. Regardless, I have been blessed to be called to put forth the effort to make the Word of God the priority of my life.

The effort I am expending to honor that call is enhanced by my increased knowledge of self. As I stated before, one of my favorite verses in scripture is Isaiah 30:21, "Whether you turn to the right or to the left, your ears will hear a voice behind you, saying, this is the way; walk in it." As I became more proficient at listening to that voice, godly attributes became more dominant in my character.

Humility now appears to be more of a virtue than a weakness. I have moved away from ego-driven, self-determined and worldly perspectives because they contradict the Word of God, in my view. Relying on God's promises is more prominent in my life now, as I lean on scripture Matthew 7:7, which states,

"Ask and it will be given to you; seek and you will find; knock and the door will be open to you." With that scripture in mind, I continue to ask, seek, and knock, trusting that I will grow spiritually.

As my ability to discern between worldly and godly influences increases, I continue on the path of renewing my mind. As my mind is renewed, the desire to look within myself, rather than seeking validation from the world. My thoughts continue to become more aligned with the Word of God, as I continue to align my life with the image of God within me. At one point, I thought I was being selfish, but I now understand that I am connecting with my truth.

God's plan provides peace and love, whereas my plan did not. It's not my job to figure out what God is doing on earth. With this understanding, I interfere with God less because I am minding my business, not trying to mind God's business. Getting to that mindset was difficult because I am human, and I want to know why things happen the way they do. So, to arrive at the mindset that everything is the will of God is hard. In my view, as I stated earlier, God is the source, not a resource. Therefore, whether I perceive something as good or bad, God is the source of it. I try to be grateful for both, the good and the bad, getting my lesson from both.

If I work at putting my heart and mind in concert with the Spirit and Word of God, my mind will be too busy focusing on doing God's work and being obedient to God's Word, rather than trying to figure out why things are the way they are. Things are the way they are because God wants them that way. My focus is on minding my business, which is to be obedient to the Word of God and waiting on God. There are two forms of waiting I would like to mention, expectant waiting (trusting that it will bear fruit) and patient waiting (remaining present in the moment). I believe patient, expectant waiting is foundational to spiritual life.

Presenting myself to God, while patiently waiting for the guidance of the Holy Spirit, with the hope that my old worldly habits change, so that I can be used for God's glory, defines my approach to the walk of faith. I no longer compromise with the world, because sitting on the fence is ineffective. Either I am in, or I am out. Selfish ambition and pride have lost their appeal. Worldly characteristics, such as pride, envy and greed, I thought gave me strength and status, are now viewed as burdens.

Though my sinful nature still exists, it is no longer a heavy burden. By walking in the light and surrendering to God's Word, I can leave my burdens at the altar. Taking guidance from the Holy Spirit, Jesus said, in Matthew 11: 28-30 "Come to me, all you who are weary and burdened, and I will give you rest. Take my yoke upon you and learn from me, for I am gentle and humble in heart, and you will find rest for your souls. For my yoke is easy and my burden is light." So, when I began working on keeping my sinful nature under control, my strength came from truth, as I leaned on the Word of God not my own understanding.

Surrendering to the idea of being guided by the Holy Spirit, meant I had to understand that God is the sculptor, and I am the clay. This shift in perspective removed my worldly pride. The idea of becoming a servant of God and the desire to see myself as God sees me became more foreseeable. I had to peel away the layers of what a life in the world had done to me spiritually. I had to surrender to God as a child, like I surrendered to the world in my youth, as I grew and matured, responding to the world with worldly values. I began to see myself as God sees me—humble and willing to serve.

Relinquishing the thought that I was in control and making things happen was hard, there were no shortcuts, the work had to be done. I committed to staying on God's path and to developing the perseverance and discipline to stay there. While I was developing the perseverance and discipline to stay on the path, the realization that I could not figure God out was becoming even more evident. As mentioned earlier, the scripture Isaiah 55:8-9, "For your thoughts or not my thoughts, nor are your ways my ways, says the Lord. As the heavens are higher than the earth, so are my ways higher than your ways and my thoughts than your thoughts," became my mantra. With that mindset I knew to humble myself and be ready for whatever God brings my way, knowing it is not for me to know why but to accept whatever it is and react using the Word of God.

God created me and God loves me. So, whatever comes my way whether it be perceived as bad or good it is from God, to shape me into the person God created me to be. As mentioned earlier, I'm grateful for both, the good and the bad, getting my lesson from both. It's all good. Getting to that understanding took a lot of study and surrender. Paul states in Romans 8:28, "And we know that in all things God works for the good of those who love him, who have been called according to his purpose." In the past, I would get upset about perceived bad things happening in my life, but with my new understanding, I know to look for the guidance of the Holy Spirit and my lesson, in every circumstance, trusting that it will strengthen my faith. My ability to be still and know that God is in the mix has been greatly enhanced.

A couple of paragraphs ago I talked about peeling the layers away of things that had built up while I was of a worldly mindset. As I began to peel the layers away, I was able to contrast and discern between my worldly existence and my spiritual life. I began to bring to the surface my God created self. I felt the key to my future was hidden in my past; every past experience was preparation for my future.

God has blessed me with insight, hindsight, and foresight. Insight is the ability to gain an accurate and profound intuitive understanding of myself. As I did the work to peel back the layers that had been accumulated over years of worldly living, my ability to discern between what is within me from what has entered me from the outside became hindsight, the ability to comprehend a situation after it has happened. Again, as I peeled back the layers of what has happened in my past, the impact of that life has had on the inside of me became known. Foresight is the ability to anticipate what will be needed in the future. With foresight, I can discern by combining what I have learned from my insight and hindsight to know what I need to do going forward.

Moving forward, doing the work to align myself with the Word of God, reconciling my past worldly life with the divine image within me. As I focused on what is within me, what I present to the world outwardly has changed. I am led to be humble and less self-confident. Having learned to be more confident in the guidance of the Holy Spirit. Self-confidence and confidence in the Holy Spirit could not co-exist, both could not be served at the same time.

The more I aligned myself with the truth the more secure I felt in the truth. Feeling secure in what I could see, and control was not the truth as I now know it. My truth had always been within me, a place that I cannot see but I now have total faith in. Standing on that faith, using my foresight and discernment, I can see the path God has laid for me.

CHAPTER 11

I'd Rather Have This

My foresight and discernment led me to desire to be more faithful to the Word of God. Looking within myself, I realized that everything I needed to strengthen my relationship with God was already inside me. Having spent the majority of my life looking outside of myself for what I thought I needed, my curiosity had misled me. Now, I understand the source of my inner conflict. By changing my focus from looking outside of myself to looking within myself brought me face to face with the person God created me to be, who I had glimpses of but did not know. As I settled into that understanding the conflict within me began to dissipate. The more I trusted that my truth would be found in the person God made me to be, the more enlightening it became.

As I surrendered to the process of sanctification, I found peace in the realization that I was not in control of my life. Though I still had decisions to make, my perspective on their outcomes changed. While I once had specific desires for the results, my anticipation of them lessened. Now, I waited for whatever outcome God had planned, accepting whatever the outcome was, whether it was my desired outcome or not, there was no stress and little anxiety. I moved closer towards the truth and the light; I began to see and feel comfortable with the understanding that God has a plan for me. With this realization, I knew I needed to get out of God's way and allow the Holy Spirit to guide me.

Taking life for granted became a mindset of the past. I became aware that not everyone wakes up each day. Waking up every morning is a gift, and I am grateful for it. As stated earlier, God cannot get any closer to me than the air I breathe. The same breath God breathed into Adam is the same air I am breathing today. I used to take those things for granted. Now, I believe that everything God brings into my life is my abundance. I have my health and as far as I know a good mind, so I am blessed.

This understanding extends to my work as a Hospice Chaplain. The gift of life is truly a blessing, and I consider myself blessed to meet people at the end of their living experience. I have met many great people as they transition out of this life, each one unique. Some people are believers, others are not, but they are all children of God. Offering a caring presence to those facing their imminent death has been some of the most rewarding work I have done.

The Lord is my Sheppard, I lack nothing and no longer trust in the world. While I still have dreams and make plans, I now take a different tone with myself as I plan. My confidence in my ability to make things happen takes a back seat to the guidance of the Holy Spirit, who directs me toward the right path, allowing things to unfold as they should. Feeling confident in and understanding that it is not me who does the work, but the God who created me, and the Holy Spirit who guides me. My job is to pay attention and acknowledge God's presence.

As I experience my salvation and transformation, I notice a welcome change within myself. Events around me no longer affect me the way they once did. I used to internalize issues and speak passionately about them. While I still have opinions, I do not internalize them. I can express my thoughts if I want to and then move on. The passion I once felt regarding worldly issues has diminished.

My understanding is, whatever happens, it is God's will and God's business. God's business is not my business, so there is no reason for me to internalize anything other than the Word of God and my ability to be obedient to that Word. That is my business; to be obedient to the Word of God. I cannot affect God's business, so; I focus on my business.

With that understanding, I recognize that both my victories as well as my failures lead me to my destiny. The knowledge I had gained from both have been invaluable. Sometimes the victories felt like answered prayers, while failures, though different, may have been answered prayers as well. At times, I still feel the need to understand why I failed. Early in life worldly values were used to make that assessment but now I am using Godly values to assess the outcome of a failure. The insight I gain by contrasting the difference between a worldly assessment and an assessment using the Word of God can be very enlightening. Now, I know to look at the motivation behind my actions, asking myself: Were my motivations and intentions, Godly or selfish?

The insights I gain from such assessments are invaluable. When I fail due to selfishness, it feels like God is disciplining me. As stated earlier, God never let me get away with anything. To avoid punishment, the only solution I could think of was to become obedient to the Word of God and guidance of the Holy Spirit.

Knowing about Jesus and the Word of God is one thing, but trusting and surrendering to it is another. In my view, knowing about Jesus and the Word of God is intellectual. Trusting and surrendering to the Word of God is spiritual. My upbringing taught me about Jesus and the Word of God as well as the idea of trusting God. But as I matured, I found trusting the Word of God was difficult because of my exposure and surrender to the world and worldly values.

My sanctification and transformation gave me the faith to trust the Word of God, which wasn't easy, but reversed my earlier inability to trust the Word of God. Years of studying and practicing stillness grew my faith and helped me to control temptations, though I still struggled with total surrender to God's Word at times. At this point in my life, I knew and trusted the Word of God, but totally surrendering to the Word of God was still a challenge. It is hard to explain, but the doubt that once hindered my trust in God's Word was gone. I couldn't figure out if it was just me being human or if I was clinging to some form of control, falling short of God's glory. But I knew in my heart I trusted God. A couple of quotes from scripture came to mind, "As a man thinketh in his heart, so is he" and "Keep thy heart with all diligence, for out of the heart comes the issues of life."

My response to the world has changed. In the past, I made little effort to resist temptation, but now I do. The level of trust I have in the Word of God and Jesus is the measure of my growth in resisting temptation. As mentioned earlier, the things I once did, I have moved away from. The stronger my commitment to the Word of God as the truth became, the more successful I was at resisting temptation. Also mentioned earlier, I had to do like Jesus when he was tempted by the devil and say, "it is written." Every time the devil tried to tempt Jesus, he would say, "it is written," meaning it is written in the Word of God. I can feel my relationship with God strengthening as I become more successful at surrendering to His Word.

Digging from under all the layers of mistakes I had made, using worldly wisdom coupled with the bad experiences I had in life, usually caused by me, was trying. But God did not allow me to quit, so, I persevered, working to correct the bad mental habits I had developed along the way. Those were the mental habits that were getting in the way of me totally surrendering to God and hampering me from getting closer to the person God had created me to be. As life continued to unfold, within me, I realized that sanctification is a continuous, lifelong process.

It was also apparent that the foundation of my sanctification is built on is solid and based on the Word of God. The foundation of the life I was living was based on worldly values, which gave me a false sense of control but lacked stability and peace. There was no peace! I was worshipping the things of the world, money, status, and position. It took time and study, but I removed my worldly foundation, replacing it with the values set before me by the Word of God. By changing my focus from an ever-changing world to the unchanging Word of God, I gained stability and peace.

Now I ignore worldly wisdom and surrender to the guidance of the Holy Spirit, allowing myself to get out of God's way. With a clear understanding of where I've been spiritually and where I want to be—developing a solid relationship with my Creator—I move forward with intention. As I study and pray, my prayers are being answered. The changes in my behavior and attitudes are evidence of those answered prayers. I now understand that the things of God are eternal and do not change, but they must be acknowledged.

Preferring the peace and stability provided by the guidance of the Holy Spirit, I believe I made the right choice, by choosing the Word of God. No more double mindedness. No longer torn between external and internal forces. Looking around, I can see the hand of God working daily in my life and in the lives of others. Why wouldn't I want to have a relationship with God?

My goal is to be aware of God's presence each day and follow the guidance provided by the Holy Spirit, daily. I know it is easier said than done, but I believe the benefits of doing this work are worth it. Everything I need to accomplish that goal is already within me. By acknowledging God's presence and surrendering to my relationship with God, I am being faithful to that relationship. As mentioned earlier, that's what God desires from me: a relationship that honors the Creator.

I cannot touch the Holy Spirit, but I can feel the Holy Spirit touching me. My awareness of spirituality is very high at this point in my journey, even though the subjective nature of spirituality is difficult to define. As mentioned earlier, the dictionary defines spirituality as, "the quality of being concerned with the human Spirit or soul as opposed to material or physical things." My communication with God has become more frequent and my relationship with the spiritual aspect of my life has deepened. My prayers come from a genuine heart, a heart yearning to commune with the soul of God residing at the center of me. Moving forward, I praise God with prayers of thanksgiving for His blessings, seeking the guidance of the Holy Spirit and wisdom to live in God's truth. I know I am covered with the grace and mercy of God.

CHAPTER 12

I Am All In

At this point on my spiritual journey, I am fully committed to my sanctification and transformation. My vocation is my spiritual life. Although the world and its temptations are still present, their ability to pull me away from God has diminished. My ego has taken a back seat to the guidance of the Holy Spirit, and my relationship with God is stronger than ever. I am grateful, but I know my work is not finished. I know I have to continue to study, pray, and allow the Holy Spirit to continue to guide me further.

Now that I have acknowledged God as the Creator of all things, my goal is to "get out of God's way." This has led me to view my thoughts differently. Changing my perspective was the most challenging part of my sanctification and transformation. Before my transformation, I rarely reflected on why I thought certain things. I knew some thoughts were not aligned with the Word of God, but I was not trying to have a relationship with God at that time of my life.

I was reactive, rather than thoughtful. When I spoke, I would "shoot from the hip" and move on. However, once I began to build a relationship with God, that approach no longer worked. My focus had changed from worldly concerns to spiritual concerns. I became conscious of my thought patterns, which had not been the case before. It is hard to explain, but my way of interacting with and communicating with people changed. I went from an "each man for himself" attitude to genuinely caring about how my words affected people. Prior to this shift in my mental attitude, I could be tactful, but, if necessary, I could also be ruthless. Before, I felt that getting what I wanted was more important than other people's feelings.

Focusing on how my words and actions affected people challenged and frustrated me. Sometimes I felt like giving up, believing I could not or would not change. But despite my failures I kept trying. It is amazing the way life unfolds. What helped me change that aspect of my communication was a stroke that affected my ability to speak. "Shooting from the hip" became a thing of the past.

By the grace of God, my speech slowly returned, but it was a long process. I had to visualize words to be able to pronounce them, which made me very aware of what I was saying. This new challenge provided me with a new opportunity to work on <u>what</u> I said and <u>how</u> I said it. Strangely, I never felt fear or despair during my recovery. Instead, I felt as if I had work to do—learning to speak again.

Having to speak slower and coping with the loss of my natural quick wittedness was tough. But I told myself that I had been blessed with being spared some of the other effects of a serious stroke. There was no paralysis or left side weakness. I had the use of my limbs. It took more than eight months, but gradually I felt comfortable with my speech.

Some years later as I reflected on my stroke experience, I wondered, had God placed that stroke in my path to help me control my impulsive speech? Was it a gift? I had taken pride in my ability to think and speak quickly, but it appeared God had a different plan for me.

While working on improving my speech, I continued to work on my relationship with God. Attending seminary required extensive reading. I read out loud to myself. I practiced pronouncing words. Three syllable words were particularly difficult; they still challenge me at times. Whenever I attempt to speak impulsively, I will stutter. I was forced to slow down and be intentional.

One of the most difficult lessons I have learned is that walking with God is a lifelong process. It takes a conscious effort all the time. There are no vacations and no days off. I believe this journey is nurtured by the love of God, and has drawn me closer through prayer, study, and worship.

Did I choose this path, or did God choose it for me? I may never know. What I do know is that I depend on the Holy Spirit to guide me while opening my heart and mind to be receptive to the path God has for my life. My desire is to see myself as God sees me. So, motivated by a sincere heart, I thank God from that place where God resides, deep within me. With faith, I know my actions will strengthen my relationship with God.

I believe that God is my source, not merely a resource. Meaning, God is the source of my spiritual, physical, and emotional well-being. My guidance and strength comes from God as well. As mentioned earlier, a life consumed by the Word of God, in my view, is a prayerful life. I now pray without ceasing. Think about it, the way we live our lives can be a form of prayer. By transforming my life into a life that honors God, I am praying. By obeying the Word of God, by loving those I encounter throughout my day and being forgiving of any transgressions, I am praying.

So, I approach God prepared to serve. I empty myself of selfish desires. I look for blessings from within. Which I believe are far better than any flesh-directed desire. As I have mentioned before scripture states, "Ask and it will be given to you; seek and you will find; knock and the door will be opened to you." God answers prayer and I expect my prayers to be answered. The answer may not appear as I expect or would like it to look, but if I pay attention, understanding will come. It is all part of God filling me with the Holy Spirit to guide me to righteousness, justice and compassion.

I have been reborn into God's kingdom, acknowledging that I am God's child. My sanctification requires that I surrender control to God. I align my free will with God's divine will. What does this mean? It means transferring total control to God. It means using my free will to do God's will. It means accepting the guidance of the Holy Spirit. As Paul said in Romans 6:22, "You have been set free from sin and have become slaves to God." This is the cornerstone of my sanctification, willfully transferring my self-determined will over to the will of God. This takes work and a daily focused effort.

It's not just talking the talk. The goal is to allow the Holy Spirit to do the interior work needed to bring my heart closer to God. As stated in Isaiah 29:13, "These people come near to me with their mouth and honor me with their lips, but their hearts are far from me." Therefore, Sunday worship alone will not work for a true relationship with God. God's presence must be allowed to invade every area of my conscious life every single day. With the Holy Spirit as my inner guide, I can walk humbly with my God.

The life of Jesus serves as an example for me to follow. My relationship with God is not based on my intellect, but on my ability to allow the Holy Spirit to transform my heart. Have you ever heard the phrase, "What would Jesus do?" That's a mindset I try to embrace as I move forward in my new life, with a new spirit, and my new set of values. Philippians 2:5 states, "In your relationships with one another, have the same mindset as Christ Jesus." In other words, I allow God to transform me into the likeness of His own son.

The demonstration Jesus set before me, is a mind of obedience that honors God in all things. Learning to walk like Jesus is a lifelong process that must be worked at consistently. It requires a change in mindset. A change from "me and I" to a mindset that recognizes that I am but a vessel through which God can work. I empty myself of old attitudes knowing, "I can do all things through Christ who strengthens me."

Walking in faith is not easy. But Jesus offers living water that nourishes my soul. What is promised from this walk is eternal life, that spiritual water Jesus told the woman at the well about. John 4: 13 "Everyone who drinks this water will be thirsty again, but whoever drinks the water I give them will never thirst. Indeed, the water I give them will become in them a spring of water welling up to eternal life."

This isn't a get rich quick scheme. Worldly success isn't the goal. The goal is the peace that comes from living a life that is based on the truth of the Word of God. God's plan is perfect. As I learn to follow God's plan, I will fail at times and fall at times. But as I put in the work to learn to follow God's Word and truth, I will fall less often and when I do fall—and I will fall—I will be closer to God when I get up.

When I get up closer to God, the growth in my faith is evident and encouraging. I know not to get discouraged. I am learning from my falls that the Holy Spirit will guide me and will be my strength as I get up. I am comfortable with the fact that my self-determined lifestyle has changed to a life dependent on the will of God. If my life is determined by the will of God, I know I will reveal what God desires of me in time. Even though God remains a mystery, my spiritual eyes have been opened. I do not have to solve the mystery. As stated in Isaiah, "God's thoughts are not my thoughts nor are God's ways my ways, God's thoughts and ways are higher than my thoughts and ways." Understanding those words, I can relax in God's presence without feelings of anxiety about God's nature.

Each trial I endure increases my faith. I trust that God is working all things for my good, because I love God. As I experience God taking me through trials and coming out refined on the other side of my trials, I have confidence that Jesus did overcome the world, regardless of appearances. Things can appear dark and bleak, but my faith assures me that hope is alive because I am alive in God and because the Holy Spirit dwells in me. My faith removes fear and doubt. I can't let the appearance of things cause me to get discouraged.

The disciples walked and talked with Jesus, yet they still faced many challenges regarding their faith and obedience. Some doubted the resurrection of Jesus, some questioned Jesus being the son of God. Therefore, I can expect similar challenges with my faith and obedience, even as I walk with the Word of God. It is God who will lead me to victory. Victory does not result from my individual strength, intelligence, or cunning. God the Creator is in control and deserves all the glory. My victory is understanding God's grace in my life.

The greatest gift I can give myself is the freedom that comes from consciously surrendering to God. By doing so, I can connect with the image of God deep within me. My sincere surrender transforms my heart and mind, clearing away the clutter accumulated from years of worldly living. I no longer seek external validation or comfort—I find peace in knowing my true self as a child of God.

That true self is the foundation I strive to build my life upon now. With unwavering devotion to the Word of God I will be able to hear the voice behind me saying, "This is the way; walk in it." My self-confidence has been transformed into Holy confidence. I am willingly following where the Holy Spirit leads me. Since I do not waver, the enemy has no choice but to turn away; he knows the power of God. As stated in James 4:7, "Resist the devil and he will flee from you." The devil's attacks are constant, and I need to be prepared every day.

Getting dressed for battle every morning, I must do as stated in Ephesians 6:13-17, "Therefore put on the full armor of God, so that when the day of evil comes, you may be able to stand your ground, and after you have done everything, to stand; Stand firm with the belt of truth buckled around your waist, with the breastplate of righteousness in place, and with your feet fitted with the readiness that comes from the gospel of peace. In addition to all this, take up the shield of faith, with which you can extinguish all the flaming arrows of the evil one. Take the helmet of salvation and the sword of the Spirit, which is the Word of God." The enemy cannot handle that, nor can he penetrate my armor.

The spiritual water that Jesus provides, is watering the roots of my soul. That place deep within me where the image of God resides. I believe that is the most important fact for me to remember: "I am created in the spiritual image of God," regardless of my physical features. I may look like my earthly parents on the outside but on the inside, I resemble God, and I need to acknowledge that by changing my perception of how I view myself. Viewing myself from the inside out, not from the outside in. My physical attributes have nothing to do with my spiritual attributes. Man looks at the outward appearance, but God looks at the heart. God's truth is the salt of my soul, and I sprinkle it.

Committing to my vocation of seeking Spiritual understanding as a lifestyle, I submit to the truth that God is the potter, and I am the clay to be formed by God's hands. Focusing on that truth, I search for the gifts, talents and abilities given to me to do God's will and accomplish the purpose God has for my life. Even though conditions may not feel or look perfect, and I may never feel fully prepared as I step out on faith, I know the Holy Spirit will guide and protect me. Remembering what is stated is in Romans 8:31, "If God is for us, who can be against us?". God is always for me when I strive to do God's will. By constantly seeking God's truth, I am bound to discover God's truth. It does not happen in an instant, but over time, with trials and challenges. Paraphrasing scripture, God has begun a good work in me by calling me into God's vineyard and the Holy Spirit will complete that work, I will produce fruit.

There is no need for me to feel anxious regarding my readiness. I can do all things through Christ that strengthens me. With the perseverance to stay the course, I have rebuilt the earthly foundation my life was built upon. The foundation I am replacing it with is solid and stable, made solid by my growing faith and knowledge of God's Word. As stated in Psalm 119:105, "Your Word is a lamp to guide my feet and a light for my path."

My vocation as a seeker of God's truth, has led to the growth of my faith, causing any doubt in the truth to dissipate and be removed from my consciousness. My faith has transformed into a conviction. I know God is real! As I search for God's will for my life, the faith that has been built within me will carry me through any frustration I feel because I know, as stated in 2 Corinthians 4:18, "So we fix our eyes not on what is seen, but on what is unseen, since what is seen is temporary, but what is unseen is eternal." My desire is to do God's will.

This understanding enables me to give God the fullness of my love, transforming my heart and mind. This transformation clears away the clutter from my heart and mind, clutter that has accumulated through my years of interacting with the world. I now choose to meditate on the Word of God. I am no longer paying lip service to the Word of God, but instead I choose to be aware of the fact that I am a branch connected to the vine of Jesus. I bear fruit, because I long to do the will of God.

I obey the Word of God with humility. Not a false humility, but authentically, without pretense. With my faith intact I commit to reading God's Word, seeking God in prayer, and fellowshipping with other believers. With an inner stillness, while going about my daily life, I seek the guidance of God's Holy Spirit to light my path. Christ has become my cornerstone, as stated in 1 Thessalonians 5: 16-18, "Rejoice always, pray continually, give thanks in all circumstances; for this is God's will for you in Christ Jesus."

The spiritual seed I have planted will grow because I continue to drink the spiritual water that Jesus provides, nourishing God's truth within me, bearing fruit which is the salt of my soul. Even though the negativity of the world is all around me and may cause me to stumble at times, if I fall, I get up closer to God. This is not an easy walk but having gained insight into the Word of God I no longer fear losing my old self but long for my new self, which is obedient to the Word of God.

Even if the world labels me a fool, I must continue to "Trust in the Lord with all your heart and lean not on your own understanding" (Proverbs 3:5).

The guidance of the Holy Spirit has led me to my true self. The Holy Spirit has connected me to God's unconditional love. I don't believe there is a greater blessing than the peace that comes from connecting with my true self. I no longer look outside of myself for comfort because I am self-reliant in knowing my true self. My true self understands that I am a child of God. That is my identity, not the person that I created based on worldly perceptions.

Obedience to God has become second nature, just as God's Word has become second nature to me. I actively seek a greater understanding of the Word of God, an understanding that lies within myself. I no longer lean on my own understanding but allow God's Spirit to guide me. I patiently wait for God's promises. This waiting is not inactivity but actively waiting while going about my daily life. There are many promises in the Bible. The one I wait for is "peace." As stated in Philippians 4: 6-7, "Do not be anxious about anything, but in every situation, by prayer and petition, with thanksgiving, present your requests to God. And the peace of God, which transcends all understanding, will guard your hearts and your minds in Christ Jesus."

God receives all the glory for my transformation. Having fed and nurtured my faith, there is no longer a reason to ask the questions, "Am I where God wants me to be or am I really following God's plan for my life?" I don't ask those questions anymore because I have decided to obediently follow the leading of the Holy Spirit to the best of my ability. I have embedded in my mind a scripture mentioned earlier, Matthew 7:7, "Ask, and it will be given to you; seek and you will find; knock and the door will be opened to you." Doubt regarding God's truth no longer exists within me as I consciously draw closer to the image of God in which I was created.

Through faith, obedience, and love, I am building my life on a foundation that will not be shaken. Christ is my cornerstone. As I move forward, I do so with confidence, fully dressed in the armor of God, prepared for the spiritual battles ahead. My identity is not in the person I once was, but in the child of God I have become. My journey is one of continual transformation, but with unwavering devotion, I know that God is leading me every step of the way.

CHAPTER 13

Can We Really Get Out God's Way?

Having accepted myself as a branch connected to Jesus, the true vine, I continue my journey. Staying consciously connected to the vine, affirms the truth of my creation, though surrendering to that truth was not easy. Staying connected took a lot of reflection, soul-searching, prayer, and study. It required years of practice to learn how to become discerning and contemplative. This led me to a profound realization: I needed to follow the Holy Spirit, not my ego.

Early in my journey, stillness did not come naturally. I was accustomed to being active, always responding quickly to life and its challenges—just as most people do. I behaved impulsively, exercising my free will. I reacted, sometimes overreacted, to situations I encountered. Through prayer, by allowing the Holy Spirit to guide me, I slowly developed an internal stillness. Now, I praise God, instead of reacting instantly to a situation, I give it time to develop. Cultivating this internal stillness has been a blessing in so many ways. When I allow the Holy Spirit to guide me, I am following God's will. When I am following God's will, I am out of God's way.

Of course, my humanness will never disappear. But I can remain mindful of God's presence within me and allow it to guide me. Acknowledging the presence of God, I have gained the wisdom to be still. Allowing my thoughts and emotions to pass without immediate reaction, and giving the Holy Spirit the lead, has been a sign of growth. That mindset serves as a guide to the path that has been predestined for me to walk.

This brings to mind a saying I'd like to quote: "I asked for strength and God gave me difficulties to make me strong, I asked for wisdom and God gave me problems to solve, I asked for courage and God gave me dangers to overcome; I asked for love and God gave me troubled people to help. My prayers were answered."

God's answer to prayer doesn't look the same for everyone. Our perceptions and needs are unique to each of us, so God speaks to each of us differently. No matter how I experience God, I must never allow myself to be separated from Jesus the true vine. Jesus left the Holy Spirit as my guide. Together, they speak to the Spirit from which I was created, the Spirit of God. With this understanding, practicing stillness and remaining aware of the presence of God becomes easier. The distractions and temptations of the world cannot alter my focus, because the one who is within me is greater than the one who is the world. Earthly things don't get to me the way they used to. I no longer stumble through the difficulties because I understand God's grace, which is truly amazing.

Grace is part of God's promise. Again, I share Matthew 7:7, Jesus states "Ask and it will be given to you; seek and you will find; knock and the door will be opened to you." My faith allows me to trust that promise. My vision and focus are on God's presence and the fulfillment of God's promises. I must have the faith to follow where God leads. God has assured me that God's presence will never leave me or forsake me, and I trust in that promise. I know God loves me and walks by my side daily.

Psalms 46:10, "Be still and know that I am God." This doesn't mean being passive or immobile; rather, it means moving forward with the confidence that, "if God is for me, who can be against me?" (Romans 8:31). My surroundings may never be perfect, but I cannot allow that to distract my focus from the presence of God within me. Staying focused is difficult at times, but I strengthen my focus by praying and meditating on the Word of God. When distractions arise, I read scripture or pray. If I am in public, I pray silently. Those around me do not need to know what I am doing.

If this sounds like work, it is, but the rewards are immeasurable. Recognizing God's presence within me is essential to cultivating a loving relationship with God. This relationship brings true peace, deep contentment, and real blessings. I do not feel burdened by my commitment to living in the truth; instead, I am filled with joy. Embracing God's way was like stepping out of darkness into light, it reminded me of my experience after Lasik surgery—when everything appeared brighter and clearer. I said to my daughter, "who turned the lights on."

Having my oldest daughter help me out was wonderful. I've been blessed with five children—three girls and two boys—who have played a very important role in my life. It has always been my responsibility to care for my family, and that responsibility motivated me to seek the best for my life. I knew I had to be a good example for my children. I made sure they understood that God and Jesus were the guiding forces in my life.

Now, my focus is on my six grandsons. I want to make sure they understand the importance of having a relationship with God and the value of prayer. I know how deeply faith has blessed my life—so why wouldn't I share that with the most important people in my life?

As mentioned earlier, Jesus has lightened my burden and turned on the lights. In Matthew 11:28-30 Jesus states, "Come to Me, all you who are weary and burdened, and I will give you rest. Take My yoke upon you and learn from Me, for I am gentle and humble in heart, and you will find rest for your souls. For My yoke is easy and My burden is light." The more I devoted myself to God and the Holy Spirit, the more I found this scripture to be true. My choices changed. I no longer made decisions that invited drama and discontent into my life. Now, my choices produce peace and contentment. Cultivating the habit of focusing on what was within me rather than external circumstances beyond my control lessened the anxiety I felt.

How I react to politics, and the news is a good example. I used to take the news personally. My peace of mind was easily disrupted. I could and would at times display emotions and contempt to what was going around me. That began to change once I surrendered to the Word of God and the guidance of the Holy Spirit.

As I became more introspective and centered on the Spirit of God within me, I felt myself opening up spiritually. My study and prayer life became evident in how I expressed myself. No longer bound by worldly influences; I refused to let past negativity shape my future. I can no longer allow my past experiences to put up barriers that close off parts of my life. Now, I strive to be more open and receptive to life's goodness daily. A quote I heard really helped me out: "Your past is a life lesson not a life sentence."

My work as a Hospice Chaplain gives me insight into how I have changed and been transformed. I am open and adaptable to whatever my patient's situation is. What I recall about myself, is how I feared death and dying before surrendering to the Word of God. But once I accepted the position as a Hospice Chaplain, I noticed a change on my first patient visit. I began the habit of praying before each visit. Asking God to "give me the presence of comfort." I visit all nationalities with varying illnesses, cancer, dementia, Alzheimer's, to name a few. Some pass away in a few days, some live longer, and some even graduate from Hospice.

My hospice experiences led me to reflect on my spiritual life. Looking back, I realized my past disinterest in spirituality stemmed from my desire to be worldly. Now, spirituality is my calling. By staying present, I recognized that true surrender to God required answering one key question: How do I relinquish my will so that God's will can guide me? While the answer is simple, accomplishing it was challenging. The simple answer was to put God's will first. By surrendering to God's will, I got out of God's way. And once I got out of God's way, I was finally prepared to answer the call in Isaiah 6:8, "Then I heard the voice of the Lord saying, "Whom shall I send? And who will go for us?" And I said, "Here am I. Send me!" That was a significant step; I knew I was different when I considered, "here am I. Send me." I had never occupied that mental space before.

Years before I became serious about my spirituality, a police chaplain shared something with me at the funeral of a high school friend. I would like to share what he told me. He said, "There are two things you have no control over, when you come into this world, and when you go out of this world. But what matters is what you do between the beginning and end." Those words made me reflect on how I was living and how I could have a more positive impact on my life and the lives of those I was responsible for. That moment was a catalyst for my transformation.

Paul expresses it well in Romans 12:2, "Do not conform any longer to the pattern of this world but be transformed by the renewing of your mind. Then you will be able to test and approve what God's will is - His good, pleasing and perfect will." Replacing worldly beliefs and habits with the truth of God's Word and the teachings of Jesus has transforming power. I believe the testing and approving that Paul refers to involves a period of reflection. As I reflected on the difference between my past life and my life now, the contrast is remarkable.

Describing the contrast between leaning on my own understanding and living with a renewed mind is difficult. It's not like I have a split personality—I'm still the same person. But I have been changed. When I leaned on my own understanding, I was impulsive, guided by my own thoughts and ideas. Few, if any, of those thoughts aligned with God's will. Although God was always in the back of my mind—thanks to my upbringing—I still put myself and my selfish desires before God. All the pleasure I chased was temporary. And like the Israelites, I faced the consequences of my disobedience over and over again.

But after surrendering to the Word of God and being transformed, my experience of life changed completely. God became first, and my desires came second. The punishment was gone because I was walking in alignment with God's will. The peace I now have on a daily basis is incredible—and nothing can turn me back to my old ways. There's no way I'm going back to leaning on my own understanding.

Most noticeable are my attitudes and reactions to the world around me. Where I once relied on my own will, I now defer to the will of God as stated in the Bible. The anger within me has dissipated, replaced by the calm and enlightening demeanor that the Word of God gives me. The will of God is indeed good, pleasing, and perfect. I submit to God's will, honoring the relationship I have been given the opportunity to nurture. Allowing my faith to grow.

Understanding that my true riches lie within me, I am spiritually prosperous, producing the fruit God placed me here to produce. By keeping my consciousness focused on the presence of God within me, I am drawn closer to God. There is no greater fruit on earth than the five children placed in my life to nurture and raise. My children have been in my life for two thirds of my journey. They have grown in the lord with me and are the light of my life.

Only God knows how truly grateful I am to have them in my life. Through them I have been blessed with six grandsons and two great granddaughters. All are being taught the meaning of faith. To God be the glory.

Scripture states in Psalm 37:4, "Delight yourself in the Lord and He will give you the desires of your heart." I have found this to be true. The Christian Walk is not easy, but maintaining the mental focus to be aware of God's presence requires a desire, and God promises to fulfill the desires of my heart. The most important desire I have is to be ever aware of the presence of God.

I once confused my own desires with those given to me by God. The difference became clear when I recognized that the desires I placed in my heart were driven by external, worldly influences. When I made the distinction between desires I generated and those that appeared without any prompting from me, I realized that God was shaping my path. My approach to each desire changed: worldly desires became secondary, while divinely placed desires became my spiritual vocation.

For instance, I once desired material wealth, equating success with status. Now, I no longer crave financial riches but instead seek spiritual fulfillment. As stated before, Matthew 7:7, "Ask and it will be given to you; seek and you will find; knock and the door will be opened to you." I no longer feel a need to devise a plan to obtain the desires of my heart; instead, I ask, seek, and knock while surrendering to God's will, trusting that God will bring the desires of my heart into fruition.

Understanding that God is my Creator, leads me to believe the desires of my heart that appeared without any prompting from me were created by God. So, my faith tells me that if I listen to the Holy Spirit which is guiding me to do God's will, I will receive the desires of my heart because I am in alignment with the will of God. Through discernment and contemplation, I pay attention and notice the changes within my life when I am focused on the presence of God. I feel that being focused on the presence of God has allowed my life to prosper spiritually. Everything I am and will be is a product of God's grace in my life. My faith has been strengthened, and I obediently follow where God leads.

Though challenges and trials still arise at times, I can follow Paul's advice to thank God in all circumstances. I rejoice and pray, knowing I am a beloved child of God. As stated earlier in James 1:2-4, "Consider it pure joy, my brothers, and sisters, whenever you face trials of many kinds, because you know that the testing of your faith produces perseverance. Let perseverance finish its work so that you may be mature and complete, not lacking anything." What once frustrated me now serves as an opportunity for growth and increased faith, leaving no room for stress. As I experienced this growth, and increased faith, my perspective on life changed, there is no reason for stress.

A life devoted to faith requires effort but becomes easier over time. Isaiah 40:29-31 assures us, "He gives strength to the weary and increases the power of the weak. Even youths grow tired and weary, and young men stumble and fall; but those who hope in the Lord will renew their strength. They will soar on wings like eagles; they will run and not grow weary; they will walk and not be faint." Not only has God given me strength, but God is always there; all I have to do is be still and listen to that quiet voice within me. That inner voice, the Holy Spirit, will tell me which way to turn, "This is the way; walk in it!"

Jesus warns in Matthew 7:13, "Enter through the narrow gate. For wide is the gate and broad is the road that leads to destruction, and many enter through it. But small is the gate and narrow the road that leads to life, and only a few find it." My life experiences have taught me that there is no reason to half-heartedly submit to my faith, the narrow gate is where I want to enter. The Word of God provides all the directions I need to enter through the narrow gate. The question is, am I willing to do the work to follow those directions?

So, my charge is to love God with all I have within me. As King David prayed in Psalms 51:10-12, "Create in me a pure heart, O God, and renew a steadfast Spirit within me. Do not cast me from your presence or take your Holy Spirit from me. Restore to me the joy of your salvation and grant me a willing spirit, to sustain me." I find that prayer to be motivating and inspiring. It speaks directly to my desire to be "ever conscious of the presence of God within me."

So, I focus on the unseen things within me. That is my faith in action. Faith, as Hebrews 11:1 declares, "Now faith is being sure of what we hope for and certain of what we do not see." Trusting in the Lord is the essence of my faith. Being obedient to the Word of God is what sustains my faith. God began a good work in me, and God will see it through to completion; I have no doubt about that. I have allowed my heart and mind to be transformed according to God's will. That was hard work, but it is not over, and I know God is not done with me yet.

A pressing question I have asked along my journey is: How can I prevent external factors from affecting the Spirit that is within me? The answer lies in vigilance, staying aware of God's presence. Scripture states in Revelation 3:20 "If anyone hears My voice and opens the door, I will come in and eat with him, and he with Me." Therefore, with an awareness of the presence of God within me, I listen for that voice and open the door when I hear it. This practice limits the effects of what I see outside of myself, not allowing what I see to have an effect on the Spirit within me. That used to be the point where I would begin to get in God's way, reacting to what was happening outside of myself.

I now recognize that what is outside of me is temporary, but the Spirit of God within me is eternal. So, I stay aware of God's presence within me and listen to that inner voice that speaks to me. Through commitment and surrendering to God's Word, my relationship with God has grown. The enemy is constantly at work trying to distract and destroy the God within me. I cannot allow the enemy to hinder my relationship with God. I have learned to protect that relationship, by letting those situations pass and looking within myself, maintaining my focus on the presence of God within me.

The times when situations cause me to doubt are over. James 2:17, warns "…faith by itself, if it is not accompanied by action, is dead". Therefore, I act on my faith, because I believe. As I have mentioned before, this journey isn't easy. I must put in the work. Acting on my faith means I am being obedient to God's Word to the best of my ability. Like anything I practice I improve at it, and it becomes easier. I believe that practicing obedience to the Word of God is no different. I bring life to my relationship with God when I obey and follow the teachings of Jesus.

My love for God is reflected in my interactions with others. Putting God first feels natural after years of keeping my focus on God. As mentioned earlier, Jesus states in Luke 17:33, "Whoever tries to keep their life will lose it, and whoever loses their life for me will preserve it." Therefore, I must empty myself of selfish desires and allow God's will to manifest within me. The love of God will shine through as I interact lovingly with those I encounter. Loving others is a very important part of Jesus's teachings.

Make no mistake, God has called me to this understanding, and I am doing my best to answer God's call, knowing that everything I need to succeed will be provided to me. I have chosen to keep my consciousness in God's presence and promises. God is not a man that God should lie, there is not a promise God can't keep because God is the creator of all things. I must overlook my weaknesses and pray for the strength to follow where God leads. God called and brought me to it, so God will bring me through it.

Viewing my life from an eternal perspective, I understand that the world as I experience it is temporary. However, as stated in 1 John 2:17, "The world and its desires pass away, but whoever does the will of God lives forever." My trials and the world will pass away just as I will physically, but if I follow the will of God, my life will be eternal. This is achieved through obedience to the Word of God as shared in Proverbs 16:9, "The heart of man plans his way, but the Lord establishes his steps." I can rely on God to guide me towards the promises in the Bible. God has called me to surrender to the word of God, but the evil one is calling me too, so I must be aware of my weaknesses. I need to trust in the power of God through prayer to give me the strength I need to succeed in my quest to be obedient. As I walk in obedience, God's purpose, not mine will be accomplished.

As stated by the prophet Isaiah in 55:11, "My Word that goes out from My mouth: It will not return to Me empty but will accomplish what I desire and achieve the purpose for which I sent it." This reflects part of the mystery of God; I do not understand how it works, but I understand that I am now walking in truth of the mystery. A truth that will bring me fulfillment and peace. By surrendering to the Word of God, I trust in the one who called me to obediently serve and share the good news. The burden I bear is not unbearable because I have submitted to God's will. God will guide me to the plan for which I was created.

Dying to myself was hard, but necessary. If I truly wanted a relationship with God, hanging on to parts of my worldly self would not serve me. Being a passionate person, I had opinions about almost everything. You name it I had an opinion regarding it. Those opinions kept me connected to the world.

As I began to process that part of my life, I realized that my opinions did not matter because I was not in a position to change anything.

Once I settled into that understanding, I realized that the world is the way it is because that is how God created it, and he created it this way without any input from me. So, what I need to do is mind my own business, which is to be obedient to the one who created me. What is amazing is that, once I settled into that mindset, my lower back pain and sciatica went away. To maintain that focus, I would recite my mantra Isaiah 55: 8-9 to myself, "For my thoughts are not your thoughts, neither are your ways my ways, declares the Lord. As the heavens are higher than the earth, so are my ways higher than your ways and my thoughts than your thoughts." That verse keeps me grounded and I can focus on working on my obedience to God's Word.

While working on one of the final edits of this book I had a great experience. As a Hospice Chaplain, I was assigned a new patient, 93-year-old Betty Wilson. After we greeted each other and introduced ourselves Betty asked me a question: Why am I still here? Then she explained to me that she was tired and ready to die. At first, I was taken aback, but I know the presence of God is always with me. So, we talked about the mysteries of the faith, and not being able to figure God out. Then I read Isaiah 55: 8-9 to her and we talked about getting out of God's way and I prayed for her, ending my visit. When I returned the next week Betty shared her thoughts regarding my previous visit with me. She had written down Isaiah 55: 8-9 and below it had written a great question: since we can't figure God out shouldn't we pray that God align our thoughts with God's thoughts? That was a profound question to me because it gave me deeper insight into a scripture I have recited for years. I have incorporated Betty's question into my daily prayer.

Remembering Aunt Reen in Tulsa Oklahoma, when she said, "Baby you can't understand the New Testament unless you know you know the Old Testament." Reading the New Testament I came across a verse I shared earlier, that supports my desire to mind my business. John 16: 33 spoken by Jesus, who tells me, "These things I have spoken to you, that in me you may have peace. In the world you will have tribulation (trouble); but be of good cheer, I have overcome the world." Again, with my logical mind I deduced that this scripture is telling me that God's ways and thoughts are higher than my ways and thoughts and his son Jesus is telling he has overcome the world, then my conclusion is, I can't figure God out and I need to listen to his son. If I mind my business and follow Jesus, I too will overcome the world, because I have surrendered to the Word of God and have gotten myself out of the way.

Somewhere around 1984, I began working on "Staying Out of God's Way," long before I surrendered to the Word God, finally embracing the Word of God in 2009. Throughout that time, after my Vietnam experience, God and I were having our internal battle; I was telling God, "You are not talking to me," and God saying, "Yes, I am." It has been said "a hard head makes a soft butt." I know God loves me because I was continuously disciplined during that time. The answer with regards to "Getting out of God's way," was right there all the time and the answer was to answer God's call.

Once I answered God's call and my transformation began, I saw obedience to the Word of God as getting me out of God's way. It became clear to me that if I was doing God's will, I could not get in the way because my actions are in step with God's will. As my desire to have control over my life dissipated and I surrendered to the guidance of the Holy Spirit, God's discipline became less because my will was more in line with the will of God.

When I committed to being obedient to the Word of God, people kept asking me, "What are you going to do?" For a long time, I would just tell them, "I did not call me, so I have no idea what I'm going to do." They kept asking me that question, so often that I grew tired of it and said what I was going to do. I can't remember what I claimed I was going to do but as God would have it, what I said I was going to do blew up in my face. That was like a revelation for me. I realized I had been right the first time, "I did not call myself, so I have no idea what I'm going to do." My mindset had been that God called me, and God would determine what I should do. My goal is to be still and know that God is God, all-powerful and in control.

While being still and waiting on God, the one that called me, what I consider to be my purpose showed up. I was minding my own business, after Tuesday night Bible study. When a friend, Harold Goodman, approached me, he told me he had an opportunity he wanted me to look at. He was the part-owner of a home health and hospice company; and he wanted me to consider being the after-hours chaplain/spiritual care counselor for his company. It did not take long after our meeting for me to accept his offer. Talk about a blessing!

Visiting elderly or sick people is something I did with my father in my youth. My father was not going to a sporting event, but he would take me with him to visit a sick friend or elderly relative. Once I started visiting patients, I couldn't believe how natural it felt. Could there be any honor greater than being allowed to be a comforting presence to a transitioning soul? A soul that has been on this earth long enough to be considered in the sunset of life or younger.

People ask me; How can you witness all that death? Amazingly enough, I truly don't see death. I see individuals in a different stage of their lives. A stage we will all have to face at some point. The amazing thing regarding hospice is, just because you enter hospice, it doesn't mean you're going to die. People graduate from hospice all the time. Early in my hospice career I saw a patient for three and a half years. She would graduate from hospice, then be put back on hospice months later. We had become good friends so when she was off of hospice, I would still visit her.

Now I no longer have to tell people, "I didn't call me! I have no idea what I'm going to do." Now I know what I'm going to do, write two books (this being the second) and be the Spiritual Care Counselor for Ace Home Health and Hospice. I am in my ninth year there.

Although the pull of the world is strong, I have been given the resolve to resist it, allowing the Holy Spirit to guide me towards the circumstances that will mold me and draw me closer to God. The salvation provided through my faith in Jesus Christ my destiny. That was the reason for the death of Jesus, to free me from the sin that kept me in the darkness. Scripture says in James 4:7, "Submit yourselves, then, to God. Resist the devil, and he will flee from you," reminding me that I am a co-heir with Jesus in the Kingdom of God. Watching God remain true to the promises, makes walking with confidence in God's truth second nature. My confidence in the Word of God has grown and strengthened my relationship with God. As long as I stay on the path God has planned for me, I will continue to move away from my sinful nature and move closer to where God wants me to be.

Remaining aware of the presence of God daily is mentally challenging due to all the input I receive from the world. However, I remember Psalm 77:11

which states, "I remember the deeds of the Lord; yes, I will remember your miracles of long ago." By paying attention and remembering all the things God has done for me and those around me, I recognize the many miracles I have experienced along my journey. There were miracles I may not have noticed or may have simply forgotten, but they occurred, and miracles are still happening today. God does not take a day off.

I can count on God to fulfill the promise God made in Jeremiah 29:10-13, "I will come to you and fulfill my gracious promise to bring you back to this place. For I know the plans I have for you, declares the Lord, plans to prosper you and not to harm you, plans to give you hope and a future. Then you will call upon Me and come and pray to Me, and I will listen to you. You will seek Me and find Me when you seek Me with all your heart." The key is for me to do my part by seeking God's presence. I must be willing to enter God's sanctuary within me, in my heart.

My mind must stay focused on God as I seek to understand through the Word of God and study how God has moved throughout history. Yet I must also give God all of my heart as I worship God despite what I see, think, or feel. Only in the sanctuary of worship, within me, will I begin to truly understand. Losing my old life is not too much to ask for receiving the benefits of God's love and grace. This understanding is enhanced by the fact that I now know I am a child of God. God will complete the work begun in me, and God's Word will not return to God void but will accomplish the purpose for which God spoke it. The love and grace of God is a gift I can never repay, but I can share it with those God places in my path.

Ultimately, I have learned that getting out of God's way means surrendering to His Word. The moment I stopped trying to control my life, my path became clear. Now, I am confident that I am walking the road God has laid out for me, fulfilling my calling with faith, love, and obedience.

I am not perfect, nor will I ever be, but I can make continuous progress concerning my relationship with God. This is evident as I have watched my actions and reactions to the world change. I know that God's promises will be kept. God will never leave me nor forsake me. I believe the peace I have received by surrendering to God didn't come from the world and can only leave me if I decide to give my power back to the world. I would like to end with a scripture from the Apostle Paul Philippians 3:12, "Not that I have already obtained all this, or have been made perfect, but I press on to take hold of that which Christ Jesus took hold of me." Be blessed as you stay on the journey set before you by God.

Appendix A

MY CREED

"I am in this world but not of it "

Jesus prays to God for himself and for those in whom he has placed the word

John 17: 14-17- I have given them the word and the world has hated them because they are not of the world as I am not of the world. I do not ask that you take them out of the world but that you protect them from the evil one.

Jesus gives us our direction and focus

Matthew 6: 33- But strive first for the kingdom of God and his righteousness, and these things will be given to you as well

Paul tells us how to avoid getting caught up and being misled by worldly values

Romans 12:2- Do not conform to the pattern of this world but be transformed by the renewing of your mind. Then you will be able to test and approve what God's will is-his good, pleasing and perfect will

Paying Attention

Jesus tells us how to renew our mind by trusting in him and the word of God

Matthew 16:25-for whoever wants to save their life will lose it, but whoever loses their life for me will find it

Jesus tells us how to increase our faith in him and the word of God.

Matthew 26:41 -Watch and pray lest you enter into temptation. The spirit indeed is willing, but the flesh is weak

Paul tells us the results of being controlled and grounded in the flesh versus being grounded in the spirit

Romans 8:6-the mind governed by the flesh is death, but the mind governed by the spirit is life and peace

Luke tells us that our heart will be where our mental focus is

Luke 12: 34- for where your treasure is, there will your heart be also

The book of Proverbs tells us to guard what we let go into our heart because what we let into our hearts will control the issues we deal within life

Proverbs 4:23-Guard your heart with all vigilance, for from it flows the issues of life.

Paul tells us how to guard our hearts

Ephesians 6:11-put on the whole armor of God, so you may be able towithstand the schemes of the evil one. The belt of truth, the breastplate of righteousness, shoes of the gospel of peace, the shield of faith, the helmet of salvation and the sword of the spirit, which is the word of God.

Appendix A

Paul tells us the results of guarding our hearts

Philippians-4:7-8-and the peace of God, which transcends all understanding, will guard your hearts and your minds in Christ Jesus. Finally,

brothers and sisters, whatever is true (real; genuine), whatever is noble (of an exalted moral or mental character), whatever is right (correct in judgment, opinion, or action), whatever is pure (free from moral taint),

whatever is lovely (of great moral or spiritual beauty), whatever is admirable (excellent; first-rate)—if anything is excellent or praiseworthy—think about such things.

Once we have all of the above, we have to have a faith strong enough and wisdom enough to

Psalms 46:10 Be still and know that I am God
2 Corinthians 5:7-for we walk by faith, not by sight

Appendix B

This day May 24th, 2000, I cease believing in visible money as my supply and my support. I view the world of effect, as it truly is simply an out picturing of my former beliefs. I believed in the power of money; therefore, I surrendered my God given power and authority to an objectified belief. I believed in the possibility of lack, thus causing a separation in consciousness from the source of my supply. I believed in mortal man and carnal conditions. This belief gave man and conditions power over me. I believed in the mortal illusion created by the collective consciousness of error thoughts. In doing so I have limited the unlimited. NO MORE! This is the day I remove my so-called humanhood and claim my divine inheritance as a being of God. This day I acknowledge God and only God as my substance, my supply and my support.

1. God will provide all of my needs. I shall not lack anything, be it spiritual, financial or happiness. Outer appearances are just that, appearances. It's the power you give appearances that makes the difference. All of my needs and desires are meant.
2. If I keep my mind on God, my true source, everything will continually be in order. I need not look outside myself for anything. I 'am, rest and exist in my being at all times. I'm whole. Continually I look inside myself for my needs are meant.
3. When I focus continually on my inner presence and truth, I feel a total freedom. I will speak from my truth on a daily basis. I can feel

nothing but good when I approach life from this view. Living from within out is the truth I will let nothing turn me around.

4. When I align myself with my indwelling spirit and acknowledge God as my source I'm filled with total confidence, and any deep-sited fears melt away. I feel the light of love and great sense of peace. From this I draw caring positive people into my life. This is where I will strive to be at all times.
5. No person, place or thing is the source of my abundance. My indwelling truth is the only source of my abundance. I will keep my mind fixed on this truth.
6. Once I let go and except things as they come, I fully understand that all my needs and desires are meet. Sometimes if I'm trying to dictate outcomes I don't understand, but if I keep my mind open it is obvious that all my needs are meet. I can feel my supply and the spirit in me welling up inside me.
7. I accept my responsibility to express the truth and acknowledge God as my abundance and source. I live with love of all; I give and share my abundance willingly. I'm in divine order and know that there are no negative outcomes. I will always look for the God presence in any situation that appears negative.
8. When I view my indwelling spirit as form, I see the light and feel totally secure. I know that all my needs are meet. The past has no bearing on my future. My life is new every day.
9. Knowing the truth of my oneness with God assures me of my abundance. I continually remind me of this truth. I await nothing for everything is in divine order. I share and give of myself faithfully. I relax and know that all is well and the will of God. I will share this knowledge with my children
10. As I have practiced many times before "I'm in this world but not of it", this is so true. Outer appearances mean nothing; it's the looking inward that expresses the truth. I give my thoughts to my indwelling presence for that is where my truth exists.

11. There is no such thing as lack because my indwelling spirit provides all my needs. My life is in order. I acknowledge my oneness with God and do not look outside of myself for anything.
12. I remain conscious of my spirit being the source of all my needs being meant. I 'am is already providing my needs and bringing all futures needs into my life.
13. My God given abundance flows freely and continuous. I will not hamper my flow with thoughts of doubt or lack. Of this truth I'm confident.
14. God is my spiritual presence, and I acknowledge and totally respond to as my source. I look to no person or thing to fulfill me because my needs are met.
15. I understand my inner presence of God, once I denounced God, when my mother left for Germany. I have never lacked, nor will I ever lack anything for God is always with me.
16. I acknowledge my spiritual source as supplying all my needs and desires. I have no concern for my needs for they are met. There is no such thing as lack.
17. I'm conscious of my responsibility to remain in the truth and not give in to the appearances of this world. There is no lack in my conscious.
18. I no longer worry about lack or use my worst-case scenario way of planning because I know all my needs are met. My God presence brings all my needs into my life as their time comes.
19. I know the truth regarding my inner source and I walk in faith with this knowledge. I give all fear and thoughts of lack to God; they do not have a home in my house. All negative thoughts come from outside and cannot manifest themselves in me.
20. When I focus on my true source I cannot see or feel the lack possible when looking at the values of this world first. The only thought before me is my spiritual presence.
21. I thank God daily for my blessings. I step out on faith knowing that all my needs are met and God is all there is. God has set my path, and I follow it.

22. No person, place or thing is my source. My source is within me. All my needs are met.
23. Knowing that my inner truth is constantly working to bring all my needs and desires into reality I relax and live life to the fullest. I'm able to share life and love with everyone I come in contact with.
24. All my needs and desires exist in me. My God self is constantly bringing my needs and desires into my reality. God is my spirit and my source.
25. My positive thoughts are my desire to fulfill my purpose. Negative thoughts appear when I lose focus of my purpose. My source is separate from both, but will bring into my life whichever one I let dominate my mind.
26. I have no wants only desires and they are made manifest in my reality in God's time, which is right on time. I have no feeling of need because all my needs are met all the time.
27. I acknowledge my responsibility to look inward to my truth for all answers to any desires I have. I know that looking outward is a not the Answer. I know that lack does not exist.
28. I acknowledge my pass mistakes of worst-case scenarios and understand that they have no place in my thought process. My focus is only on the positive aspects. I no longer give into the negative scenarios I create mentally and so it is.
29. I'm aware of God being my fulfillment and I have no anxiety about life because all my needs are met. I look outside of myself for nothing.
30. My focus is on being in this world but not of it. When I look outside myself, I know I'm setting myself up for disappointment. I'm always in the right place at the right time and in the right situation. God leads me to make the correct decision.
31. I know that abundance is mine. I relax and let God work. I follow Gods lead and know that all needs are met. I'm thankful for God's grace.
32. I know worry has not place in my life because my source is the God presence within me. This is my daily focus, as all my needs are met.

33. I acknowledge my inner presence of God as my source. I realize that prosperity includes al aspects of my life, health, peace of mind, answered prayers and shelter. For all these things I'm grateful.
34. I'm very relaxed in my knowledge of God's presence in my life. I need entrust nothing to God because God is already in control and I'm led by divine guidance.
35. I'm at peace knowing that all my needs and desires are met right now and forever. When my conscious mind tries to doubt my knowledge, truth takes over clams any negative thoughts.
36. Worry has no place in my house because all my needs and desires are already and constantly met. I'm abundantly provided for.
37. I acknowledge God as my source and I handle my responsibility with regards to that acknowledgement. My responsibility is not to give appearances any power in my life.
38. The past stays in the past. With my new and correct understanding of the truth. Mistakes of the past will not be repeated. I need have no anticipation of the future for all my needs are met.
39. I now understand the truth and the errors of my past thought patterns. God has and will always provide all my needs and desires. All I need do is rely on my faith in the spiritual presence. As I relax and watch my life unfold, I see my desire manifest in my life. God is all there is.
40. To these 40 days I'll be faithful. God is all there is and constantly brings into my life what I desire. Nothing or no one can change my faith. Love is all there is and God brings love into my life daily.

www.ingramcontent.com/pod-product-compliance
Lightning Source LLC
Chambersburg PA
CBHW071119160426
43196CB00013B/2632